Noumenautics:

metaphysics – meta-ethics – psychedelics

Essays by
Peter Sjöstedt-H

Published by
Psychedelic Press
London, UK

Copyright ©2015
Peter Sjöstedt-H and Psychedelic Press

ISBN: 978-0992808853

Cover design and typesetting by *hobgobgraphics.com*

For more information:
www.psychedelicpress.co.uk
www.philosopher.eu

*Dedicated to my
Anja, Arthur and Isolde*

Contents

Preface

Noumenautics: from *nous* and *naus*, the Ancient Greek terms for *mind* and *ship*. The word noumenautics is born too from Ernst Jünger's term *psychonaut* in its connotation of psychedelic exploration, and from Immanuel Kant's term *noumenon* in its connotation of an unperceived reality. The *psykhe* of psychonaut denotes more the soul whereas the *nous* of noumenaut denotes more the intellect, thus one might say that the noumenaut is a philosophical psychonaut – one who navigates through both the human harbour of ideas and out through to the inhuman ocean that is psychedelic consciousness.

Yet that harbour is not necessarily a haven. This collection of essays and notes, seemingly heterogeneous as they are assembled from a number of publications, all share a sharp critique of prevalent beliefs. The metaphysics used from multifarious thinkers all veer towards a panpsychism: that sentience, in its various modes, exists not only through complex physiology but in fact in all forms of reality. This metaphysical claim is tempered from mawkishness by a meta-ethics, in this case a nihilism. From Nietzsche and others is forged a thoroughgoing view of moralities as power structures, with those structures being fortified and conditioned by a metaphysics of will. It is the essay on Nietzsche's use of psychoactive chemicals that steers us out to the Atlantic abyss of psychedelic phenomenology.

I use phenomenology in the sense of the general study of phenomena, of experience. For philosophers of mind, phenomenologists of any school, and indeed for all those interested in consciousness, the psychedelic experience offers the supreme impression. To deny philosophers of mind psychedelic substances is tantamount to denying instruments to musicians. If one is to study consciousness, one must involve its most wondrous manifestation. Who would read a study on the nature of music written by one who had never heard any pieces composed before the 21st century? This book therefore attempts to introduce considered philosophical analyses of the psychedelic consciousness. Also documented is my personal report and analysis of ingesting Psilocybe fungi: a most positive life-changing event.

I am more than aware that my philosophical interests in metaphysics, nihilism and psychedelic phenomenology are each somewhat rare in the field. Furthermore, in combination one could say they present a singular breed. It has been my life's purpose to harmonize these ostensibly disparate strands, and I see this book as offering an inception into that attempted harmony.

For this book I should like to thank Robert Dickins, the editor of Psychedelic Press UK, for his support and editorial skills, my parents and brothers for their nurturing of independent and philosophic thought, and my Anja and our children for their perennial love.

Peter Sjöstedt-H

September 2015 – West Cornwall, UK.

I

Philosophy and Psychedelic Phenomenology

Due to the general legal prohibition and modern cultural taboo against psychoactive chemicals, the academic discipline of Philosophy has left a potentially bounteous field of enquiry virtually unharvested. The aim of this text is to introduce readers to an unimaginable universe of cognition to which ingestion of such molecules opens the portal. This universe can modify and augment Philosophy itself: psychedelic phenomenology is fuel for Philosophy.

One of the most natural and planetarily prolific of the psychedelic substances is that from the so-called 'magic mushroom'. There are more than a hundred known species of such fungi, the majority of these containing the psychoactive molecules psilocybin and psilocin, which are structurally similar to the brain's serotonin. A notable exception is the faery-tale red and white Fly Agaric mushroom, which contains the psychedelically-active molecule muscimol.

One of the most common of the psilocybin fungi is the Liberty Cap, or *Psilocybe semilanceata*. With its pointy cap, this little fellow looks like a pixie wizard. It is found abundantly throughout the Western world and beyond. As well as being amongst the most common it is also amongst the most potent of the psychoactive fungi.

An intake of more than forty or so Liberty Caps can bring one into what seems to be another realm. Although the effects vary amongst persons, certain features remain somewhat constant in this enthralling state of *psychedelic phenomenology, or 'psy-phen'*. At first one feels lightheaded, and light: gravity seems weaker. One begins to lose bodily coordination skills, as if one were returning to toddlerhood. With one's eyes open, objects seem to sway, often rhythmically; things seem to pulsate, sometimes vehemently. Flowing patterns are registered, colours fluctuate and become vivid, foods offer supreme tastes far overreaching one's previous benchmarks. And all of this is further transcended when one closes one's eyes: here one travels through what appear to be galaxies, one meets apparitions, insectoid beings, spriggans, spacecrafts that try to communicate, perhaps thus more microscopic protist organism than artificial vehicle. One experiences feelings that are novel, and therefore ineffable – without words existing to which they could refer. 'Normal' emotions can increase in intensity; perceptions, concepts and feelings can become intertwined and thereby lose distinctness as such. Time can seem to oscillate in rate, space loses meaning – one enters a most fascinating mode of experience, which after five ('normal') hours or so departs.

One obvious field to which psy-phen applies is the Philosophy of Mind. Neuroscience can be included within this field, but the area mostly involves itself with broader, yet often convoluted, questions that relate to how the mind can be understood within a wider worldview that might incorporate metaphysics, language, evolution, and other disciplines that provide groundwork, anchor-points, for explanations – rather than the mechanistic groundwork of most neuroscience. One sub-category of Philosophy of Mind is 'phenomenology' which, in the sense used here, is the study of reality from the initial standpoint of consciousness, or what Immanuel Kant called 'phenomena'. This in contradistinction to studying the world as if the objects we perceive exist precisely as they are perceived by us humans, with our particular biased ways of perception. That phenomenology as it exists today has virtually excluded any study of psy-phen is akin to zoology excluding any study of mammals.

Until somewhat recently Logical Behaviourism dominated the Philosophy of Mind. This is the view that consciousness does not exist, but that language deceives us into believing that it does. In fact, it contends, all mental terms – such as 'happy', 'angry', 'curious', 'belief', etc. – merely refer to physical behaviour, not to mental forms. One of the rationales for this Behaviourism was the fact that states of consciousness cannot be empirically verified, only their physical correlates can. I cannot empirically perceive your happiness, but I can perceive your smile. This is ultimately based on an epistemology (theory of knowledge) that asserts that anything that cannot be empirically verified cannot be known to be true, excepting mathematics and logic. This limiting epistemology has a long history but came to prominence at the start of the 20th Century under the name Logical Positivism. After undergoing psy-phen, one realises the absurdity of Behaviourism: whilst practically motionless, without any behaviour, a 'psychonaut' can traverse unimagined starscapes, become an animal or other creature unknown, undergo feelings that do not belong to humans, and so on, *ad infinitum*. That all of these mental experiences are really forms of behaviour is as implausible a view as believing Santa Claus to be an insect.

More generally, materialistic explanations of mind seem to become less feasible after psy-phen. Perhaps the body is not moving, but surely the brain is highly active somehow *causing*, or *being*, these psy-phen experiences? Well, in philosophy and biology there exists the so-called 'Hard Problem of Consciousness'. This is the problem that no matter how well one understands the processes of the brain and the nervous system as a whole, one still will not thereby understand how physical movements cause, interact, or are identical to, conscious states, or 'qualia': *how physiology causes or coincides with phenomenology.* Dopamine activity may be correlated to the qualia of satisfaction, but a material physiological study will only show one that physiological activity is occurring, it will not show one the process whereby that activity is translated into the feeling. Especially since the work of the French philosopher, René Descartes, we have focused explanations on the reduction of everything to matter and mechanism. With consciousness that mode of explanation reaches its limit. As the great British philosopher Bertrand Russell put it,

> there will remain a certain sphere which will be outside
> physics ... it is obvious that a man who can see knows
> things which a blind man cannot know; but a blind man
> can know the whole of physics.[1]

Fundamentally, any explanation is founded upon one's epistemology. One's epistemology is closely linked to one's sense of identity, and thus epistemic disagreements often become heated as they circumnavigate the personal. Psy-phen often allows one escape from the epistemology inculcated throughout one's life. The marvels of nature become wondrous once more because they do not automatically get swept into pre-formed epistemic categories of thought (such as 'leaf', 'building', 'painting', and so on). A 'leaf' can offer an awe-inspiring delight of vision, with its nexus of veins, its reservoir of green tones indicating its sublime photosynthetic machinations.

One notion within our contemporary paradigm of belief is that consciousness is necessarily conditioned by a brain: no brain, no mind. However, under psy-phen this idea seems less tenable. The French Nobel laureate philosopher, Henri Bergson, made the argument that the brain filters consciousness to one's bodily requirements, but that the brain does not create consciousness. This would imply that decreased brain activity could actually mean increased, raw unfiltered, consciousness. Recently, such an inverse correlation has been observed.[2] Bergson drew the analogy between a radio and the program it was playing with a brain and the consciousness linked thereto: damage the radio or brain, and one can have correlated programmatic or mental damage, but this does not logically imply that the radio produces the program or that the brain produces the fundamental essence of consciousness. Bergson's contention that memory, as an aspect of consciousness, was not dependent on a brain has recently been to an extent corroborated by the discovery that slime-mould – cousin to the fungi – has a memory despite, of course, not having a brain.[3]

The argument here is that psilocin, etc., acts by inhibiting brain activity thereby increasing mental activity, generally speaking. An implication is that consciousness, or at least a basic form of subjectivity, is an aspect of all organisms, not merely the more complex animals – i.e. that plants, fungi, etc., have basic forms of consciousness. This view is known as panpsychism. The great mathematician and philosopher, A. N. Whitehead, argued that all of existence was actually living, there being no difference in kind (but only degree) between what is commonly distinguished as the organic and inorganic. His 'philosophy of organism', or Process Philosophy, can be summarised in his assertion that 'biology is the study of the larger organisms; whereas physics is a study of the smaller organisms'.[4] This does not mean that tables or cables have their own subjectivity, but that the partly self-organising ('autopoietic') entities that compose them do, from organism, to cell, to molecule, to atom and beyond. Such a philosophy, linked to hylozoism (the philosophic notion that all is alive), may very well seem preposterous to a person with an epistemic base rooted in post-Cartesian thought. This is essentially because it transgresses the axioms that uphold that thought. But as Friedrich Nietzsche stated, 'rational thought is interpretation according to a scheme we cannot escape'.[5] We think that mind is conditioned by brain, but this has never been proven. Strictly speaking, we cannot even prove that other people have minds, known in Philosophy simply as 'The Problem of Other Minds'. Technically, to assume that the mind is caused by brain due to psycho-physical correlation is to commit the fallacy *cum hoc ergo propter* hoc (correlation does not imply causation). Psy-phen opens one to novel lanes of thought seemingly incredible in a contemporary normal state of mind – a mode of being that could not be closer to the philosopher's remit of questioning all axioms, uncovering all assumptions. As Nietzsche's precursor, Arthur Schopenhauer put it,

> *Philosophy has the peculiarity of presupposing absolutely nothing as known; everything to it is equally strange and a problem.*[6]

Panpsychism and its ilk does not of necessity imply Dualism: that mind and body are two separate substances. Schopenhauer argued that the world was composed of subjective 'wills', or drives, desires, that were merely represented by us humans as spatio-temporal matter. Thus matter as such is caused by our human form of subjectivity, rather than human subjectivity being caused by matter (as brain). Matter and mind, in this form of what is known as Transcendental Idealism, are both aspects of a single reality (Monism), rather than the belief that two substances interact (Dualism), as is common to many religions.

Schopenhauer was a follower, with important qualifications, of the great Prussian philosopher Immanuel Kant. Kant is known as instigating the 'Copernican Revolution in Philosophy'[7] because he argued in a most rational way that we do not perceive objects as they actually exist, rather objects exist in the way they do because we humans automatically 'translate' a given world into forms conforming to our minds' structures. Thus, reality is divided into *phenomena* and *noumena*: how things *appear* and how reality actually *is*, respectively. For Kant, even space and time were not real but were projected by us onto the real, the noumenal. In this sense, perceived 'everyday reality' is the hallucination. As Einstein wrote,

> *I did not grow up in the Kantian tradition, but came to understand the truly valuable which is to be found in his doctrine ... only quite late. It is contained in the sentence: "the real is not given to us, but put to us (by way of a riddle)."*[8]

One frequently reported occurrence in psy-phen is the strange contraction and dilation of the speed of time: a minute can seem an hour; an hour, a minute. Space, also, distorts in unexpected flows – both of which conduce the idea that psy-phen is interfering with the normal functional mode of mental projection, perhaps allowing the person to gain a glimpse of noumena, the 'real reality' not encaged by absolute space, time, or other categories of mental projection. Kant believed that humans could not access noumena, but perhaps psy-phen is a key.

Schopenhauer drew out the consequences of the view that space and time are not real, namely that reality cannot have spatial or temporal distinctions: no past or future, no here and there. Fundamentally all is one – the study of which is called henology. This view has a tradition going back at least to the ancient Greeks, and especially to the neo-Platonist thinker Plotinus. Schopenhauer applies this metaphysical insight to his ethical theory. For him, compassion was the intuition of this underlying henology, and this was thus the basis of his ethical theory – thereby linking the two philosophical fields of metaphysics and ethics. In fact, psilocybin is beginning to be seen as an ethical, therapeutic 'medicine' with universities now beginning to report on its great potential in a number of areas including the treatment of depression.[9]

Psy-phen certainly can suggest this ethical approach that deifies compassion, an emotion that can be pushed to intense levels in this state. However, such pleasantries should not be overstated with regard to psy-phen. There exists also what can be called the dark psychedelic state: visions of horrific, Bosch-like spectral demons and vast shadow-cast alien expanses, to express but a fraction of this empyrean hell. To a certain extent, these dark visions and concomitant feelings are a part of what is called the 'sublime'. A couple of centuries ago there was much discussion regarding the 'beautiful and the sublime', triggered by William Smith's 1739 translation of an Ancient Greek book on the subject by Longinus. Under psy-phen, one's aesthetic sense is greatly intensified. Objects usually shunned are suddenly appreciated for their astonishing beauty, be this natural or artificial (even that distinction often breaking down in the state). The sublime was described by Edmund Burke to be a feeling of delightful awe caused by some possible terror. In psy-phen, this sublime can then approach. It can be feared or it can be relished – this is probably in part dependent upon one's character and indoctrination.

If one has been brought up in a typical western religious setting, such sublimity might be met with an adverse reaction. Indeed Edmund Burke, in his book on the topic,[10] quotes Milton's portrayal of Satan[11] as an exceptional example of the sublime. In psy-phen one can at least ostensibly become the figures one perceives. The sense of self can also disintegrate in this state, opening up further questions about identity. A number of thinkers have suggested that the psychedelic state is identical to the mystical state. This suggestion alone makes psy-phen invaluable to the Philosophy of Religion. When one reads the mystics' accounts, their experiences often seem indistinguishable from that of psy-phen. A mystic's religion will influence the interpretation of the experience, but the substratum is recurrently of the same kind. A luminescent figure can be interpreted as an angel, a deva, an alien, a ghost, a faery, and the like, but the figure with its apparent telepathy remains as such. There are many theories regarding the origin of religion, it is certainly viable that the intake of psychedelics such as the magic mushroom is one of them. This was Aldous Huxley's view in his essay, 'Heaven and Hell'. If you were offered a natural pill that could give you a mystical experience – a taste of heaven and hell – would you take it? But be aware that this is not a 'party drug' – it is of a different class. It is highly potent and involves the risks mentioned above with regard to altering one's mind, in a philosophical sense. In a physiological sense, psychoactive fungi were recently found to be the least harmful drug, much less so than alcohol and tobacco.[12]

Hence we end with Political Philosophy, and consider the assertion of the 'Father of Classical Liberalism', John Locke: the end of law is not to abolish or restrain, but to preserve and enlarge freedom'.[13] That, for instance, a fungus shown to pose no danger to health, in fact conversely shown to have therapeutic properties, as well as having great academic import, that such a fungus that commonly grows in local pastures is prohibited by threat of severe punishment by many nations – even listed as a Schedule 1 drug by the United Nations – is an affront to human dignity and an affront to reason itself. It is certainly a restraint on the freedom to expand one's mind. Psychedelics no doubt ought be revered rather than feared, respected in the former manner. We must alter the current impression of them, and allow psychedelic phenomenology to once more enter the academic field of enquiry.

II

Myco-Metaphysics:
A Philosopher on Magic Mushrooms

This report and reflection of my, 'my', experience of magic mushrooms begins on a walk with my brother through paths and fields in an isolated Cornish landscape. It is late October and the weather is particularly foggy. We turn into a grazed set of fields facing north. I was later to discover that this set of conditions is considered the ideal for the occurrence of the most common, and amongst the most potent, magic mushroom on this planet: *Psilocybe semilanceata*, or, the *Liberty Cap*.

Fortunately my brother was an amateur mycologist, and so immediately recognised the distinctive appearance of these little fungi: a cream colouration throughout the thin, crooked stem and the bell-shaped cap. Most distinctive, though, was the 'nipple' apex. We spent a few hours gathering a hundred or so specimens. At home, I placed them to dry and began reading about the organism, chiefly to gauge the safety of its ingestion.

A few days later, on a Sunday afternoon now in London, I mix about fifty of the 'shrooms' into three pots of yoghurt, to avoid their earthy taste. My girlfriend is with me in our flat – it is important that she is in my company as a loving anchor to reality, 'reality', as my studies indicated that deep fear can arise in rare cases.

After an hour, not much has occurred. I feel somewhat light, but not much else. I read the newspaper, but lose interest. Half an hour later, I begin to feel disappointment because I am not experiencing the effects I had read others experience. But now a drunken state befalls me and I simply want it to end. If I had wanted to become drunk, I should have enjoyed the taste of a fine beer as well, rather than the muddiness of dried fungus. As a result, I have a slight anxiety simply to return to my usual state of mind. But then I decide to consider this anxiety as a phase of the trip I realised was now, near two hours later, emerging. The anxiety left and the journey began.

I should say now that this new state of being consisted of a variety of quite different phases, both mentally and physically (if I may for now use that standard dichotomy). It was as if I had taken several distinct drugs one after the other, although certain features were constant such as spatial and temporal distortion. The first phase in fact began with spatial distortion. I looked at the printer whilst sitting at my desk – it seemed to expand slightly, then retract, as if (I think now) it had a ribcage and lungs within so to breathe. I then turned to the right and stared at a lit paper lampshade. Its two-tone yellow texture suddenly became three-dimensional, having a depth of a centimetre or so. Fantastical interwoven streams flowed thereon, resembling a choreographed serpent dance or an animated Celtic, Nordic and Saxon weave design, as witnessed on historic jewellery and weapons. It is speculated that the Vikings at least took another hallucinogenic, or entheogenic (enThorogenic), fungus – the Fly Agaric – which induced the berserker rage where the warrior became one with his wolf or bear shirt ('*ber-serk*').   ♦

Next, I stood up but noticed that I had lost some control of my body. My body weight now seemed to match that of a lunar walker; my mind, of a lunatic. I floated to the sofa, slumped down and closed my eyes. I was overcome by a rich, deep, warm, loving calmness. I felt more comfortable than I had ever felt in my thirty-odd years of life. An incident of the 'sublime' began on that sofa: I softly fell through a gigantic tunnel that had a diameter of miles, a tunnel filled with golden cloud somewhat reminiscent of candyfloss. Next to the tunnel was a similar but smaller tunnel that was somehow to the upper left of my vision. Certainly I experienced the sublime, but it was combined with a feeling of supreme warmth and bliss. I felt as if I were in a channel that transported beings between the different celestial cities found in a heaven. Here too, time distorted in the sense that I did not know whether I had immersed in this calm for a few minutes or a few hours.

The next step through the wardrobe revealed what seemed to be a portal to yet another reality. What I experienced with my eyes closed far exceeded what I experienced with those wide-pupilled eyes open: the most awe-inspiring patterns and spacescapes, perpetually in motion. I witnessed gigantic, multicoloured layers, now and again becoming more directly three-dimensional. It is difficult to describe, but sometimes a three-dimensional image became properly three-dimensional, such as the difference between seeing a three-dimensional object on television and seeing it in everyday reality. At that point, 'I' felt as if it were therefore 'real' (though I shall qualify that personal pronoun and adjective later).

In this inner world, where I felt as if I travelled through the universe, I at one point arrived at a superstructure of pointy luminescent sheets that converged at a centre point, like a star-sized, wide mechanical rose. This structure was a sentience, however; an alien being who tried to communicate with me. I here thought that perhaps (I was not certain) our search for alien life was restricted, as humanity was only looking for it in the eyes-open world, the world Immanuel Kant calls *phenomena*. Rather, we should realise that this other world I was accessing was the one that aliens used to make contact. Again, I was aware that I was speculating and certainly did not have the conviction of certainty that William James labelled *noetic* for mystical experiences. I did not know; I considered. But, as epistemology reveals, we cannot know, be certain of, much at all even in the phenomenal world. Even the great empiricist David Hume understood the problem of induction and causation which afflicts the science of men. A wishful thinker could have easily interpreted his experiences here as evidence of aliens, or even of God. The question concerned the veridicality (objective reality) of that which was experienced, and thus the fundamental nature of consciousness.

An early twentieth-century dominant school of thought, Logical Positivism (or Verificationism) would confer absolutely no veridicality upon such experiences. James' notion of noeticism would be shot down by the Positivists' 'Verification Principle', which claims that a statement can only be meaningful if it is either true by definition or if it can be verified by the senses. Alfred Jules Ayer was a notable and vociferous advocate of this school, explicitly applying it against any knowledge claims made by mystics. Many people still today harbour, unwittingly, this Verificationist ideology: if it cannot be proved, it cannot be true. However, Logical Positivism itself was forced to move on – due, ironically, to logical problems. When asked later in life, in the late 1970s, what the main shortcomings of the movement were, Ayer replied, 'Well ... nearly all of it is false!'[1]

Later still, a year before his death, Ayer had a (near-/)death experience. He wrote about it in an article in the *Sunday Telegraph* in 1988 entitled 'What I Saw When I Was Dead' – and though it was brought on by pneumonia, it might as well have been brought on by psilocybin. He wrote that whilst clinically dead, he

> *was confronted by a red light, exceedingly bright, and also*
> *very painful even when I turned away from it. I was aware*
> *that this light was responsible for the government of the*
> *universe. Among its ministers were two creatures who had*
> *been put in charge of space. These ministers periodically*
> *inspected space and had recently carried out such an*

inspection. They had, however, failed to do their work properly, with the result that space, like a badly fitting jigsaw puzzle, was slightly out of joint.

He later in the article remarkably remarked that,

On the face of it, these experiences, on the assumption that the last one was veridical, are rather strong evidence that death does not put an end to consciousness ... my recent experiences have slightly weakened my conviction that my genuine death, which is due fairly soon, will be the end of me, though I continue to hope that it will be. They have not weakened my conviction that there is no God.[2]

Interestingly, one of the main issues with Logical Positivism was the so-called 'Problem of Other Minds': how can I really know that other people, other beings, have minds? Of course, we assume that others have minds; but we cannot strictly prove it, we cannot verify it. We cannot, as it were, perceive the consciousness of another, despite perceiving their behaviour. Even with a brain scan, we can only infer (rather than experience) that a person has a mind – a very useful inference. Therefore, a statement such as 'He decided against it' would have to be meaningless for the Verificationists. Instead of abandoning belief in such everyday statements, most Positivists abandoned their creed.

However, this really led to the abandoning of one sinking ship for the embarking upon another fatefully leaking vessel: Behaviourism. If a statement such as 'You are satisfied' cannot be verified, some hardliners reasoned, then it must be because such statements do not refer to states of mind but merely to behaviour. Thus entered the prevalent Western academic notion that the mind, or consciousness, did not really exist. All statements about conscious states could be reduced to statements about behaviour. For instance, if someone said, 'I am happy', that happiness could ultimately be reduced to physical movements such as smiling, laughing, etc. There is no happiness, only behaviour. This seemingly incredulous ideology pleased many in the scientific field because, as the proverb goes, science would be happier if consciousness did not exist. Well, with this Logical Behaviourism, it did not exist. Neuroscience could steam ahead without being concerned with 'consciousness', now on a par with alchemy and alien abduction.

Apart from the ease it caused a lot of researchers, it also harmonised with a larger ideology that still prevails: Materialism: that each and every phenomenon can be essentially reduced to 'things' moving in space-time according to 'fixed laws'.

As the water started to flood into the Behaviourist vessel – mockingly reflected in the quip Behaviourist greeting, 'You're fine, how am I?' – a more serious crack manifested on the hull in the late 1990s: 'The Hard Problem of Consciousness'. This was really a centuries-old problem that had reasserted itself due to the implausibility of this Behaviourist modern paradigm and its materialist relations: Eliminativism, Functionalism, etc. The Hard Problem of Consciousness is that no matter the extent of knowledge concerning the brain and nervous system, one will never from that be able to sufficiently understand consciousness. 'Things' moving in space and time (*viz.* neuronal transmitters, ionic pulses, etc.), no matter the complexity, will never yield a knowledge of the consciousness which is, no doubt, correlated to that movement. Knowledge of movements cannot amount to knowledge of *qualia* (experience). As Frank Jackson once put it, in not so few words, a brain expert who has never experienced the qualia of redness will never gain a knowledge of redness through having a total knowledge of brain anatomy and function. Experience transcends neurology.

If I studied the activity of the brain of an octopus, two-thirds of which lie in its arms, I might gain an understanding of how certain physiological activities result in certain other physiological activities, such as neuronal pattern A relating to behaviour A. However, no matter how much I materially investigated, I would never actually know what it was like to be that octopus, to know how it experienced life. Logically speaking, it is not even necessary that eyes correspond to vision, or that ears correspond to sound. Even to human synaesthetes, these common correspondences do not attain; they can hear colours and see sounds. That the psilocybin of Liberty Caps is dephosphorylated to psilocin, which then mimics the effects of serotonin in the brain's serotonin receptors, etc., tells me little about the experiences correlated thereto. Even equipped with a total understanding of how psilocin acts upon the brain and body, one could not sufficiently know the experiences taking place because many such experiences are unknown, novel and because of this ineffable; and thus cannot be reported – and for mind-brain correlation, one needs that correlate: the mind report. Even if an octopus theoretically gave a report of its teuthological *qualia*, we humans would be none the wiser: there is even recent evidence that such cephalopods can 'see' with their skin.[3] Moreover, as I shall later mention, it may very well be the case that the brain does not completely produce the mind (that it does is an unproved assumption based on conflating correlation with causality). Knowledge is not reducible to moving matter.

This is to say, the Hard Problem of Consciousness can be seen as a disproof of Materialism.

With this in mind, one can be more open to the offerings of psychedelics. In fact, furthermore, psychedelic experience should be welcomed by researchers in the fields of philosophy of mind and neuroscience, as it once was in psychology, as it can present such awe-inspiring, unusual states of mind – an untapped ocean. To go beyond a mere physical understanding of the mind, to a thus metaphysical understanding, can be practically catalysed through these fungi. *Magic mycology is practical metaphysics.*

At one point a few hours into my magic myco tour, I noticed a cup of tea sitting in front of me as I lay on the sofa. I wanted it, but my desire found it very difficult to direct my body. Slowly I managed to move towards that hot drink, I crawled up to the table and demanded my body to at least sip the cup.

Whilst this overall tea motion was in play, a myriad of other thoughts, feelings and bizarre visions enveloped me. Most of these experiences were indescribable, I'm not even happy dividing the experience into that triad of words. If only the Behaviourists had tried such psychonautical substances, they might have realised the impossibility of their faith. How possibly could the behaviour that was the slow clumsy tea crawl executed by my body in any way translate into the psychedelic experiences I was having en route? In fact, for most of my voyage I was not behaving at all: I was lying still, eyes closed, traversing the universe, conversing with occult elves, insectoid aliens, deities–

God: I saw two flowing eyes staring at me. I considered them sentient and I still felt bliss. If I were already religious, I should probably have considered this to be proof of God. However, I realised that if I had not the cultural understanding of God from religion, I could not have interpreted my meeting as one with the Almighty. Secondly, as has been said of dreams, what really is the difference between dreaming that one met God, and actually meeting God in one's dream? There seems to be no experiential difference, either in dreams or during psychedelic experiences.

I could equally have interpreted this as a meeting with aliens desperate to make connections with human beings, or I could have interpreted it as a demon, or even as Satan. A spiritual experience must still be interpreted, and the tools used for interpretation are significantly cultural. The question though is whether religion emerged from such experiences in the past, or whether religion emerged from power structures, ancestor worship, anthropomorphism, linguistic twists, etc. I should argue that what we now call religion has a plurality of origins, drug-induced experiences being but one.

Writing of the devil, at one point I believed I was the devil, Satan himself. This was because, I think now, I saw many occult, demonic images but felt completely at ease; as if the dark spirits were my friends. One image I remember in particular was a sort of waterfall, shaped as a goat's head, from which fell and ran tens of wolves, goats and skulls towards me. It was in black and white, but covered simultaneously in multicolour. At another point, I saw a streaming wall of skulls and iron crosses. It was hell; but I liked it, I was at home here. So it dawned on me that I was probably the Prince of Darkness. I took this all very light-heartedly, despite the intensity of the images. Perhaps there was no real distinction between gods and devils – in Revelation 22:16 it states that I, Jesus, am Lucifer (Lucifer being the Latin for bringer of light, Venus). It was only post-biblical theologies that interpreted demons as the old pagan gods, Lucifer as the Devil, the fallen angel. As Nietzsche advocated, once we think in terms beyond good and evil (a dualism introduced by the Zoroastrians, advanced by the Christians), we will be able to interpret in a purer fashion. Dark demonic imagery is not necessarily 'evil'; a so-called 'bad' trip may only occur to those with deeply inculcated cultural value distinctions. If one is able to accept both creation and destruction as necessary elements of reality, one can accept life. In Jungian terms, to accept oneself involves accepting the Shadow archetype – a notion inspired by Nietzsche's strand of nihilism and Freud's similarly influenced 'Death Drive'.

Before I opened my eyes and entered the world of phenomena once more, another ostensible realisation dawned upon me: What was 'me'? I realised that what 'I' am/is, is only one 'thing' as a word. Really, 'I' is a conglomerate of many levels. Though I had come to this thought previously in life via the study of Kant, Nietzsche, and some psychology, I had never properly come to this feeling. At one level throughout the trip, I always considered reason to be there, as a judge, a viewer of what was happening to me. Though reason had lost his power over the body and was very easily sidetracked *vis-à-vis* 'his' line of thought. I considered reason as something that rolled on the underside of my skull, metaphorically. On another level was the unfolding of 'my' imagination. If this was merely imagination, it was also 'I' that was its author. But then on another level still 'I' – another 'I' – was watching this imagination unfold. Parts of the mind were watching other parts of the mind, so what part was 'me'? The Ancient Greek view that one watches a dream rather than has a dream would make this realisation less perplexing.

Another level still of my self was my body. As I opened my eyes, I decided
to try reading. Rather surprisingly, when I opened Nietzsche's *Thus Spoke
Zarathustra*, the first sentence I encountered was, '"My ego is something that
should be overcome": that is what this eye says.'

I was now moving a little more fluidly, normally. However, not all was
as it seemed.

Not only was space being made a mockery of, but also time. As I waved
my hand before me, it left a trail of itself. As I followed a lemniscate path
with my hand, a lemniscate figure remained. The reason for this, it seemed
to me, was that the present, the now, had extended its duration. What I saw
and what I 'remembered' seeing were combined, giving the impression of a
trail. The now had expanded to around five seconds – recent memory was
perception, or rather perception and memory were not particularly distinct. It
was not Schopenhauer's 'Eternal Now', but it was a longer now.

The great philosopher Henri Bergson's main ideas concerned time and
perception, the mind and memory. Aldous Huxley employed Bergson's
thought in his text, *The Doors of Perception* – probably the most celebrated
psychedelic text in the athenaeum – wherein he describes and interprets
his mescaline experiences in the 1950s, a time when such pharmaco-
psychological adventures were seen in a more respectable academic light;
before the prohibition imposed in the 1960s blacklisted this field of study, to
the detriment of the advance of man.

For Bergson, all outer perception involves the contraction of memory:
for example, the colour red is partly a collection, a contraction, of billions
of certain electromagnetic waves. Without 'memorising' the initial waves,
the latter would not engender the redness. It seemed as if this automatic
human memory-for-perception function had allowed more of the past into
the contraction with regard to my lemniscate trail. Other life forms may
very well have other durations of memory for perception, thus perceiving
the universe very differently from we humans. This would entail perceiving
time at relatively different speeds, a notion recently acknowledged in the
scientific literature.[4] The magic mushroom, in other words, grants one entry
to non-human modes of time and sensation. And it is worth noting that there
is no absolute, correct, real 'speed of time'. Nietzsche, when explaining the
philosophy of flux as advocated by Heraclitus, illustrates strikingly this time/
speed variability:

> *The inner life of various animal species (including
> humans) proceeds through the same astronomical time-*

space at different rates ... [Reduce] sensation threshold by one-thousandth ... then every four hours we would watch winter melt away, the earth thaw out, grass and flowers spring up, trees come into full bloom and bear fruit, and then all vegetation wilt once more ... a mushroom would suddenly sprout up like a fountain. [Decelerate more] the solar ecliptic would appear as a luminous bow across the sky, as a glowing coal, when swung in a circle, appears to form a circle of fire ... Whatever remains, the unmoving, proves to be a complete illusion, the result of our human intellect ... forms exist only at certain levels of perception.[5]

Bergson argued that the brain did not produce the mind, but merely channelled it according to human practical requirements – a theory that would still entail mind-brain correlation in scans. The brain would hence be a necessary but not sufficient cause of standard *homo sapiens* consciousness. Therefore, mind would be antecedent to brain, and far overreaches the limited versions of consciousness that are useful to our survival and development. It is the practical will that determines the extent of human consciousness – thus if one theoretically closed the will, one could thereby open the doors to that greater overarching mind. Applying Bergson's dense theory,[6] one can say that psychedelics act as will inhibitors, they breakdown the normal functioning of the brain, so that consciousness is not restrained in this way. In other words, psychedelic compounds do not only produce 'hallucinations' (everyday reality also being a hallucination, in the strict sense), but they also allow access to a reality usually denied. It would not be in our interest to be constantly awestruck by sublime celestial cloud tunnels and so on. In this light, psychedelics can be seen as a temporary death; as such Ayer's near-/ death experience, above, resembling a psychedelic experience, is made sense of.

Furthermore, in Bergson's thought there is no actual distinction between the subject ('me') and the object ('it') because a perception exists in both, as a perception is one process that is ultimately indivisible, even at the bodily limit. A perception of a star is both part of that star and part of you, the process of its light entering and adjusting your body is one process; the consciousness lies throughout, not merely within the brain. However, it is in our biological interest to dissect reality into parts so that it can be manipulated through reason: medicine and weapons lying at either end of this practical spectrum. But these useful abstract distinctions (words such as 'me', 'star', 'perception') can be annulled through psychedelic intake, thus providing an intuition of unity, empathy, identity, etc. – a common unifying, henological insight experienced not only in the psychedelic state but also in mystical states.

But the ultimate unity of all does not contradict the overall multiplicity of power structures. An organism must exploit its environment to live: it must digest external organisms, re-constitute the atmosphere through its breathing, and so on. The psychedelic experience can provide one with intuitions of both aspects of reality – there is no moral hierarchy in total acceptance. The transcendent unity must interweave with the immanent Nietzschean *Wills to Power*.

At a later point, I started writing notes, quite odd as I look at them now, in order not to forget my trip. I noted that art and logic were essentially the same thing, in that they put 'things together, under a scheme (composition in art, taxonomy in biology)'. This seemed somewhat profound at the time, but now seems a little shallow. However, I do believe that this idea and others could be investigated further, and therefore realise that the fungus liberated my thoughts enabling seeds to be sown for development when the mind is less free but more focused. The term 'Liberty Cap' is hence quite fitting for such mushrooms – fungi for Philosophy.

III

Psychedelics
and Empiricism

Western thought is dominated by the epistemic philosophy of Empiricism, notably advocated by John Locke and David Hume. Concisely, Empiricism claims that thoughts or ideas are copies of human experience, specifically of two main types: impressions of sensation (sense perceptions) and impressions of reflection (inner feelings). Thus all knowledge is based upon this experience interpreted through reason; there are no other avenues to knowledge.

However, it seems to be the case that this Empiricism is disproved by the existence of psychedelic consciousness. I shall seek to prove this by responding to the question:

Can psychedelic experience (psy.ex.) be classified as:

(a) Impressions of sensation?

(b) Impressions of reflection?

(c) Ideas?

With regard to:

> (a) Impressions of sensation are traditionally understood as sense perceptions, that is that which is delivered through the eyes, ears, nose, mouth, and flesh.

>> **i.** Psychedelic experience is notably visual but with eyes closed. Thus the psy.ex is *not* an impression of sensation as such.

>> **ii.** Psy.ex. can certainly augment an impression of

sensation, but the augmentation is separate from that initial phenomenon which is augmented.

(b) Impressions of reflection are traditionally understood as inner feelings such as love, hatred, desire or will.

> **i.** Impressions of Reflection are thus not visual, thus psy.ex., being notably visual, *cannot* be classified as impressions of reflection. Psy.ex. does include feelings, but it is not this alone – it is broader.

(c) Ideas are traditionally understood as copies of impressions, 'less forcible and lively'[1] copies as compared to the original impressions. The idea of anger is less lively than the impression of anger. Imagination is considered a complex of such ideas.

> **i.** Psy.Ex. is *not* of necessity a copy of antecedent impressions, because of its content: this is glaring to those who have undergone psy.ex. as it is often novel and ineffable.
>
> **ii.** Psy. Ex. Is *not* a copy of antecedent impressions, because of its lively immediacy: it is not a memory but a forcible present impression (though not one of reflection or sensation).
>
> **iii.** It may be argued that the psy.ex is simply complex ideas, augmented from former simpler impressions (as in Hume's examples of the golden mountain and the virtuous horse[2]). But this criticism *fails* because:
>
>> **1.** The psy.ex. is not a copy of impressions, but itself lively impressions (see (c)ii. above).
>>
>> **2.** The psy.ex.'s contents are often excessively novel and thus ineffable, as can be directly proved during psy.ex. The mystical otherworldliness of psy.ex. can far transcend that of dreams.

Thus, psy.ex. cannot be classified as an impression of sensation, impression of reflection, or as an idea.

We could say that psy.ex. is a *third type of impression*, incorporating yet fundamentally transcending the other two. The essence of this transcendence can be said to be the ability to liberate the creative power of the mind beyond the impositions given by sense and normal human experience.

Hence, psy.ex directly contravenes the empiricist David Hume's central claim that

> *though our thought seems to possess this unbounded liberty, we shall find, upon a nearer examination, that it is really confined within very narrow limits, and that all this creative power of the mind amounts to no more than the faculty of compounding, transposing, augmenting, or diminishing the materials afforded us by the senses [first type of impression] and experience [second type of impression].*[3]

Those limits are broken by psy.ex: thoughts gain excessive liberty.

The human mind is more powerful than Hume realised. And this power ultimately disproves his philosophy of empiricism because of its claim that all knowledge be based on normal human experience (the two types). There are further possible routes to human knowledge.

To be fair, Hume did consider the possibility of non-human impressions and ideas,[4] dreams and madness. But all of these had little effect upon his empiricism except to add a skeptical qualifier thereto.[5]

Locke and Hume were concerned with refuting the 'Rationalists', such as Descartes, who argued that there existed 'innate ideas' with which we are born[6] – ideas such as that of God. Now, psy.ex. as a third type of impression does not *ipso facto* necessitate such Rationalism over Empiricism. The psy. ex. (at least ostensibly) introduces novel thoughts and feelings, etc., rather than realising innate ones.

However, psy.ex. does enable us to realise that our knowledge is not limited to impressions of sensation or reflection; our thought is not in fact 'confined within very narrow limits' but can be at great liberty.

Ultimately, terms such as 'impressions', 'ideas' etc., are crude abstractions from the flow of consciousness, and as abstractions do not concretely describe reality. The reality is far more intertwined. Indeed, these abstractions can be more easily identified as such under psy.ex. Essentially the distinction between ideas and impressions is artificial. My purpose here was merely to offer another criticism of Empiricism which has been neglected, employing local terms.

Postscript:

I recently came across a harsh quotation from the opium-psychonaut Thomas De Quincey (1785 – 1859) against the Empiricist John Locke, a quotation perhaps inspired by De Quincey's psychedelic phenomenological knowledge:

> *[If] a man calls himself a philosopher, and never had his life attempted, rest assured there is nothing in him; and against Locke's philosophy in particular, I think it an unanswerable objection (if we needed any), that, although he carried his throat about with him in this world for seventy-two years, no man ever condescended to cut it.*
>
> (*On Murder Considered as One of the Fine Arts* [1st paper])

IV

Bergson and Psychedelic Consciousness

Outline

The main points I wish to convey in this brief text:

1. That all existence is movement: 'Process Philosophy'

2. That language is extremely useful because it is extremely misleading

3. That the understanding has evolved for practicality (power) rather than for knowledge

4. That brain does not produce the mind, despite neural correlates of consciousness

5. That the observer *is* the observed; (that subject and object are partially one)

6. That mind is ubiquitous: 'Panpsychism'

7. That fundamental reality is metaphysical creativity – *and* that this can be intuited through psychedelic intake

In effect, I shall endeavour to show that the re-emerging 'Process Philosophy' of Henri Bergson *et al.* offers a potent lens through which the psychedelic state can be understood.

Process Philosophy

Process Philosophy is a term notably addressed retrospectively to the philosopher Henri Bergson (1859–1941), and to the Cambridge philosopher-mathematician, A. N. Whitehead (1861–1947) who explicitly borrowed some of his ideas from Bergson. Bergson emphasised the fact that if we consider any so-called object we realise that it has no definite boundaries *in space or in time*. For instance, a 'mushroom' constantly changes its form, and is in fact one with its mycelia (roots), which in turn is one with the nutrients 'it' gathers in the substratum, etc. There exists no clear boundary. Even with more durable objects, if we accelerated time and saw them over eras, we would see mountains fluctuate like waves in the ocean. Contrariwise, so-called atoms and molecules also fluctuate, as we now know.

That language is extremely useful because it is extremely misleading and that the understanding has evolved for practicality (power) rather than for knowledge

It is language, or more specifically words, which cut out of the fluidity that is reality, isolated 'things'. This isolating process (differentiation) serves the human species very well: in order to predict the future and to create tools/ technology (for our survival and development), we need to assume that there are stable 'things' so that we can put them into a model, and apply to these things stable 'laws'/'constants', and expect from these practical results. And though this method of extraction and *hypostatisation* (solidification) yields the produce of *science* (medicine, weapons, etc.), we must realise that this natural method is merely a model of reality, not reality itself. As both Bergson and Friedrich Nietzsche (1844–1900) stated, through divergent lines of thought, we are all inbuilt *Platonists*: we mistake concepts for reality. We are especially prone to geometrical conceptualisation, mistaking fluid reality for the motion of stable things in a pure geometric space. Plato is himself the gaoler of his famous cave – escape from which may be effectuated through psychoactive intake, as we shall see. In reality, things and space are *one entity*: movement/becoming/change. It is difficult for the human species to think of movement without thinking that some *thing* must exist which moves (e.g. water in waves), but that is simply a result of our evolved natural mode of thought. We must ontologically prioritise movement over 'things that move'. It was the abandoning of the theory of aether as the substance underlying the movement of *electromagnetism* that led to Einstein's paradigmatic theories (via Maxwell). We even like to split time into 'things': *instants*. We thereby think of time as separate from (equally separated) 'space', 'matter', 'forces', and so on. Due to our practical geometric bent, we think of this differentiated time as instants on a spatial line. But an 'instant' as such cannot exist because it must have a beginning, and an end, and therefore a duration. This abstraction, this differentiation, is a mistake that leads to Materialism and Determinism: i.e. that reality can be *reduced* to 'things' (corpuscles) which act according to timeless laws ('constants') which can be thus theoretically predicted instant-by-instant. We have abstracted from experience elements which never existed separately in reality, and then we have tried to put those elements back together again to concoct phenomena such as consciousness as an *effect* (i.e. epiphenomenon) of these abstractions. Whereas in truth consciousness was *already* present prior to that abstraction effected throughout experience. This illusion is useful to mankind, yet it is *mistaking the model for reality*. Time, space, matter, force, etc. are all one phenomenon in experience, they are divided in analysis – but we must bear in mind that the analysis is artificial rather than natural. The purpose of Philosophy, according to Bergson, is to think beyond this human condition of useful analysis.

In summary thus far, there can be no 'instants' (a mistake due to the spatialising and division of such spatialised time). There can be no 'things' (a mistake due to isolating repetitive movements away from their continuations). There can be no known 'laws'/'constants' of nature, due to the *Problem of Induction* (from David Hume): the natural belief that the unobserved resembles the observed – a necessarily non-provable axiom.

Therefore: we must acknowledge that our understanding has evolved for practicality rather than for pure knowledge. We must understand that illusion serves us well, and realise that other creatures will have their own modes of thought, useful for them – their realities thereby no doubt differing widely from ours (*à la* Thomas Nagel's question, *What is it like to be a bat?*).

That brain does not produce the mind, despite neural correlates of consciousness

Due to this, our evolved practical mode of thought, we are naturally inclined to *reduce all phenomena to things-moving-in-time* (rather than the reality of pure movement). This is then Materialism, or Mechanism. So when addressed with the phenomenon of *consciousness*, it seems natural to reduce it to material things moving in the variable of time. Such a belief has a long history, stemming back at least to the Atomism of Leucippus and Democritus two and a half thousand years ago.

Today, more specifically and especially, consciousness is presumed to reduce to neurons firing impulses and molecules to one another within the brain.

This error (of confusing model for reality) is further entrenched within the modern mindset due to the additional error of confusing correlation with sufficient cause or identity. It is believed by many that because consciousness is correlated to brain activity (in brain scans and in brain damage), the brain must either sufficiently *cause* consciousness (epiphenomenalism) or be *identical* to consciousness (identity theory): often referred to through the notion of 'neural correlates of consciousness'.

But from correlation to cause or identity is a *non sequitur* (it does not logically follow) because, analogously, as Bergson points out, there is also a *perfect correlation* between a radio set and the program it is playing. Change the radio's circuitry and you will change the perceiving of the program. One could even predict/read the program from investigating the radio's circuitry. But, of course, this perfect correlation does not imply that the radio sufficiently (totally) *causes* the program! Neither does the perfect correlation imply that the radio *is* (identical to) the program. In fact, in this case, the radio merely picks up and translates the program, which has its source elsewhere. This is analogous to the ultimate Bergsonian view. That analogy seeks to show that mind is *not necessarily* brain, or caused by the brain. Another old, but recently revived argument, shows that the mind *cannot* be sufficiently understood by the examining the brain: the 'Hard Problem of Consciousness'. That is, that 'things' (molecules, pulses, etc.) *moving* according to procedures ('laws') can never yield the full understanding of any knowledge of subjectivity. For instance, dopamine levels may be correlated to the feeling of satisfaction, but no matter the complexity, satisfaction cannot be fully understood by a mere analysis of matter moving. There is a huge chasm between matter moving and qualia (experienced qualities). As Bertrand Russell stated, 'It is obvious that a man who can see knows things which a blind man cannot know; but a blind man can know the whole of physics. Thus the knowledge which other men have and he has not is not part of physics.'[1]

These problems are only problems for Materialism. The problems emerge due to the original mistake of extracting from the flux of reality, separate (artificial) parts in terms of space, time and force. It is as if someone looked at a cake, extracted all the tones of colour from it, then painted it using those colours, believing that with a precise enough duplicate the painting would eventually have all the properties of the original cake, including its taste.

**That the observer is the observed
(that subject and object are partially one)**

Thus, if brain is not mind, what is? Bergson employs his Process Philosophy (that *all* is process, becoming, movement, change) and argues that the perception we have of 'something' is *actually a part of that something as well as a part of 'oneself'*. There is a continual uninterrupted flow. (Obviously the words 'something' and 'oneself' here are used metaphorically at this point, as ultimately are all words.)

Consider, say, looking at a star. If we trace the actual elements involved in this *process* we understand that electromagnetic waves of a certain frequency move towards us, this light then transforming through the eyes' lenses hitting the retina, transposing into an ionic pulse through the optic nerve to the occipital lobe, thereafter continuing to virtual (possible) bodily actions via the whole nervous system, etc.

The words 'star', 'eyes', 'brain', 'nervous system' seemingly present these concepts as isolated parts which may interact with each other. The reality is, Bergson argues, that these are all one system, with artificial cuts (necessary for utility). There is no absolute distinction between the eye, the brain and the nervous system. *So why isolate consciousness at an artificially-created part of the entire flow (at the brain)?*

Furthermore, why isolate the 'eye' from that which it perceives? The eye and the electromagnetic frequencies it redirects are part of *one process*. And the electromagnetic frequencies are part of the *star* from which they emanate, again there being no absolute distinction.

In other words, *the observer is the observed. Part of the star, and my perception of the star, are numerically identical (the same thing).* (All words in that sentence being mere artificial extractions from a single flowing reality.) That part of the star that is my perception of it, is the part that *evolution* has *extracted* for the practical purposes of me, the human. That is, my perception of an object, and part of that object, are one. They lie in the relation *part-to-whole* rather than in the relation *representation-to-object* (the latter is commonly believed not only by Materialists, but also by Cartesian Dualists, Kantian Idealists, and indeed most of western intellectual history).

Immediately before Aldous Huxley refers to Bergson in his well-known text, *The Doors of Perception*, he writes (of his mescaline experience),

> *I spent several minutes – or was it several centuries? – not merely gazing at those bamboo legs, but actually being them – or rather being myself in them; or, to be still more accurate (for "I" was not involved in the case, nor in a certain sense were "they") being my Not-self in the Not-self which was the chair.*[2]

I believe the passage expresses well a more direct intuition of our part-to-whole relationship with our environment, purified from common conceptual consciousness.

If one damages or alters part of the brain, part of the process is altered, so a concomitant alteration in mind would ensue; but likewise, alter the process elsewhere, outside the body (for example, cut the emanating light with a cloud) and the consciousness will also change. *If one scanned the brain during a star-gazing session, one would expect to find a perfect correlation between the neural correlates and the reported vision, according to Bergson's hypothesis that the brain does not produce consciousness but is merely a centre for the redirection of incoming signals (frequencies) to virtual (potential) bodily actions.* Again, such neuroscientific correlative data does therefore not by necessity suggest a materialist explanation. Technically, to assume that the mind is caused by the brain, due to psycho-physical correlation, is to commit the fallacy *cum hoc ergo propter hoc.*

This purpose of the *brain,* for Bergson, to direct incoming data to possible (virtual) bodily movements, gives us *power* over our environment. It is not to produce consciousness, but only to *streamline* it to practical considerations. The activity of the brain is the continuation of the movement of 'external objects' within us, so to be able to further that movement to our own purposes: in line with Nietzsche, this is ultimately to develop power over our environment.

Further to perception being a part of the 'object', Bergson states that all perception includes *memory.* For instance, to see the colour of an object involves contracting innumerable electromagnetic waves into one's 'present'. Therefore, *consciousness is essentially memory, as there can be no consciousness without a contraction of the past.* And as the brain does not produce consciousness *per se, memory is metaphysical.* It is well to note at this point that memory has been demonstrated in certain plants[3] and slime-moulds,[4] thereby indicating the fact that memory is not dependent upon a brain.

For Bergson, the past always exists in its entirety; it is the brain that limits its recollection to practicalities, and brain damage that limits its reception, that is, its effectiveness for action. In dreams, Bergson writes, when the mind is not immediately concerned with its physical environment, the past is more open to revelation.

That mind is ubiquitous: 'Panpsychism'

So, if the brain is not sufficiently responsible for consciousness, and it is only the inbuilt Platonism of our understanding that lets it seem that it is – but yet that consciousness *exists* (which is the most certain fact that one can have, beyond any scientific 'fact'), then the implication is that this flow, this movement, this becoming that is *pure reality* is itself a form of consciousness (which is memory).

Panpsychism, that all is mind, is accepted (to an extent) by Bergson, Whitehead and an increasing number of western thinkers. Bergson thinks consciousness, or subjectivity to be more precise, exists throughout *life*, organisms, whereas Whitehead argues that subjectivity is ubiquitous, including crystals and molecules. *Not* that they believe, say, a table *per se* to be conscious: Bergson confines subjectivity then to organisms, and Whitehead confines it to 'actual entities' and 'societies' (self-organising systems: the molecules that make up the table have a subjectivity in themselves, basic but there). Whitehead calls his thought the 'philosophy of organism', arguing that 'biology is the study of the larger organisms; whereas physics is the study of the smaller organisms.'[5]

Although panpsychism, or panexperientialism, may seem *prima facie* unbelievable to many, it must again be realised that the currently popular paradigm of Materialism has reached a *cul-de-sac*: to believe that mind is a product of matter, produced by the activity of artificially differentiated elements of reality, can only lead to the Hard Problem of Consciousness, Solipsism, and a profusion of mind-matter paradoxes.

That fundamental reality is metaphysical creativity and that this can be intuited through psychedelic intake

Bergson argues that underlying our human mode of experiencing reality exists a metaphysical domain of pure creativity. One method by which he argues for this is through the examination of evolution. Bergson showed the problems inherent within Lamarckism and neo-Darwinism, involving the problems associated with mechanism, determinism and teleology, and offered an alternative theory ('creative evolution') whereby a vital principle strives through matter to expand itself to full consciousness. Mankind is at the pinnacle of this vital drive (*élan vital*), but he makes room for the emergence of the superman, not too unlike the theories of Nietzsche: a being who has supreme power over his environment as he can contract more of reality into qualitative elements.[6]

This metaphysical creative domain is difficult to grasp through the intellect, but Bergson emphasises the fact that it is a mistake to believe that *intellect* is the only means to knowledge. He opposes this path to that of *intuition*, which though very difficult to pursue (as it opposes our human practical condition), can yield many advances. This is because, by transcending the 'cut-up' falsely differentiated world proposed by the intellect, it allows for many former problems and paradoxes (such as Zeno's) to be seen in a pure light, as it were – his own philosophy perhaps being a prime example.

Now, by subduing the mechanism of our nervous system, psychedelics seem to be a route of entering this state of *intuition*, uniting with this metaphysical creative domain by disassociating from the practical *will*. Psychedelics are the consolation to Bergson's lament with the route of human evolution:

> *Consciousness, in man, is pre-eminently intellect. It might have been, it ought, so it seems, to have been also intuition ... A complete and perfect humanity would be that in which these two forms of conscious activity should attain their full development.*[7]

Let us elaborate on this psychoactive process. The ingestion of certain substances (e.g. psilocybin, mescaline, dimethyltryptamine, lysergic acid diethylamide) disrupts the everyday workings of our brain and body generally. As the brain does not produce consciousness, neither do these substances directly produce psychedelic experiences. These substances rather act by hindering normal physiological functioning by inundating relevantly susceptible synaptic clefts, thus neurons and so the nervous system as a whole. Due to this disruption, memory – which as mentioned cannot be physical – can no longer act effectively for the body: the connection between incoming perceptions cannot follow the usual physiological lines and so it is not properly contracted by memory into the stable objects we would normally experience. Instead, our consciousness/memory is, as it were, freed from having to act in a practical manner. As well as the resulting loss of articulate bodily motion, this results in a number of avenues of fresh phenomenology, experience. With eyes closed, our memory, now dislocated from bodily action, retreats back into the pure mental or metaphysical realm which consists of memories of experiences and that domain of pure creativity which, for Bergson, guides art, evolution, paradigm shifts, creative thinking generally and in fact the free advance of the cosmos itself. The psychedelic experience accords with this as trips can be both personal and radically novel: impersonal and shocking in their ineffable sublimity. Theoretically, the higher the dose, the more the physiological disruption, and so the further from the personal will the experience become, as memory will be further dislocated from bodily action to which personal memories pertain.

With eyes open in this state, an abundance of unusual phenomena take place. The continuation of objects within our physiology is either halted or haphazardly passed through where possible, dependent again on dose (high to low, respectively). A table may seem to fluctuate its shape and size, for instance. Furthermore, because memory is dislocated, such an object may not be recognised as such, as 'a table', and accordingly it may not even be registered as a distinct 'thing'. Here we can understand that psychedelics can return us to a pre-analytic comprehension that excludes artificial separations ("table"), i.e. *intuition*. Further still, the artificial separation between subject and object can be overridden and a sense of unity with the so-called objects can be intuited, as quoted from Huxley above.

As various wavelengths will no longer be contracted to form our common qualia ('redness' from certain electromagnetic frequencies, etc.) because memory has lost its grip on our body (and thus environment), colour changes can occur, as well as those qualia of the other senses. Moreover, this also implies that our common sense of time may not be processed in the usual way: if, for example, we can contract fewer waves into a sensation, our present would be a longer duration compared to an everyday duration of the same 'objective' time (though even that Newtonian notion is rendered obsolete by the Theory of Relativity). Bergson explicitly distinguishes *duration* from *time*, the former being the lived-in experience, the latter being the physicists' artificial time line (T_1, T_2, etc.). Ultimately, there can be no absolute standard duration as an artificial moment (T_n) cannot *per se* determine its experienced duration. Other creatures indubitably experience different durations to us: a fly perhaps considering our human motions preposterously slow. The psychedelic experience can allow us into these different modes of duration, providing potentially fascinating inhuman phenomenology.

Another aspect of the psychedelic experience is that of finding objects, which in sobriety are often overlooked, immensely beautiful and fascinating, especially 'organisms'. This is, in opposition to the eyes-closed entrance into the pure memory/creativity province, a contrary movement away from pure memory towards the object of which you are always a part. The nervous system is not functioning as it has evolved to function, abstracting from the environment useful extracts. Now instead, it can perceive an object with less practical bias and so really feel the fuller essence of it, also part of itself – *less extraction and more absorption.* Further still, in accord with panpsychism, as all organisms have a subjectivity (a basic consciousness) it is not impossible that one can enter into these otherwise-alien minds – diffusing into the panpsychic universe.

The divergent avenues that can be experienced under the psychedelic state are of course dependent on various factors such as substance type, the dose, the person and his/her current mindset and physiological status, the current milieu and environment, preconceptions, inculcations, and more.

In sum, the psychedelic experience in not simply abstract hallucinations caused by chemicals in the brain, but rather the diffusing of the individual consciousness into the larger reality and into alternative modes of being. *It is the ordinary everyday consciousness that is the hallucination in the sense that it is but a mere fractional-practical perspective of reality.*

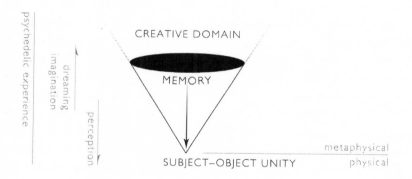

V

Vertexes of Sentience:
Whitehead and
Psychedelic Phenomenology

Introduction

Psychedelic experience, or psychedelic phenomena (psy-phen), and its study, psychedelic phenomenology, has in our culture traditionally been deprecatingly deemed as a risk-laden dice with death or madness, or, contrariwise yet impudently, as a comico-quirky brain epiphenomenon of little consequence. Both approaches to psy-phen are woefully wrongful routes and block its true significance: psy-phen can be an experience of inhuman aesthetic heights which embraces the sublime and the beautiful, and can transcend to dimensions still further. Psychedelics' hazard to our health is minimal; the history of their prohibition and condemnation grounded not in wisdom but in politics.

Of all academic disciplines, philosophy has foregone most potential gains by abnegating psy-phen. That a discipline immersed in consciousness should avoid this most multifarious and deeply rich form of consciousness is regrettable. There has been a recent revival in psychedelic studies generally, and much interest is focused upon new neuroscientific findings of the effects of psychedelics on the brain. Though this is a fascinating and necessary line of research, I shall argue in this essay that we cannot expect this line to lead to a comprehension of psy-phen. By using the ever-influential verdant process philosophy of Alfred North Whitehead – with a little help from Schopenhauer, Bergson, James and Nietzsche – *I shall seek to interpret psy-phen as a phenomenon not of mere recreation but as ingression into the workings of empyreal creation.* Through this process rendition of psy-phen, we aim to fulfill Whitehead's definition of philosophy:

> *[T]he essence of great experience is penetration into the unknown, the unexperienced ... If you like to phrase it so, philosophy is mystical. For mysticism is direct insight into depths as yet unspoken. But the purpose of philosophy is to rationalize mysticism: not by explaining it away, but by the introduction of novel verbal characterizations, rationally coördinated.[1]*

Whitehead's Cosmology

Whitehead's mature philosophy can be seen as a detailed and advanced systemization of ideas intuited and intellectualized notably by Henri Bergson and William James. The exposition of this new system does require 'novel verbal characterizations', that is, a new vocabulary and syntax, because of the implicit metaphysical connotations in current philosophic parlance. We shall begin by an exposition of what Whitehead calls his *Philosophy of Organism*, known to many as *Process Philosophy*, and thereafter examine the place of psy-phen within this system.

Due to the purported failure of science in its materialist, or mechanist, form, Whitehead presents a *philosophy of Creativity*. Mechanism seeks to explain reality through the theory that everything can be fundamentally reduced to what we understand as matter-energy operating according to the fixed laws of nature. New fundamental entities may be discovered but they may not be created. Thus, the future is theoretically determinable had one the comprehension and intellect, à la Laplace's demon. Heisenberg's Uncertainty Principle may blur the determination, but it is still deemed an eternal principle that cannot add novelty to the universe, only cloud its determined possibilities. In opposition to this mechanist creed, Whitehead develops his philosophy of creativity.

For Whitehead, the universe is constantly creating novelty rather than running a determined path. The universe creates a path in its stead; it does not drive along an already created track. It is in this sense more plane than train, more thrust than rail. The 'laws of nature' are merely regularities observed and reified by us after their occurrence. A mistake of mechanism, or science, is the *fallacy of generalizing from the particular*: that an event be regular does not entail that it be constant. The laws of nature may change, new laws may be created[2] – the universe is potentially infinite in its creative capacity. Due to the mechanist assumptions that inform its method, science cannot explain phenomena such as consciousness, teleology, causality, memory, and novelty as opposed to change of the same. As Whitehead puts it,

> *Science can find no individual enjoyment in nature:*
> *Science can find no aim in nature: Science can find no*
> *creativity in nature; it finds mere rules of succession ...*
> *They are inherent in its methodology. The reason for this*
> *blindness of physical science lies in the fact that such*
> *science only deals with half the evidence provided by*
> *human experience.*[3]

Human experience provides us with knowledge of a world of emotions, purposes, and other experiences that could only be understood as trivial epiphenomena by a cosmology that initially excluded them by abstraction and simplification. *Whitehead argues that* experience *is a fundamental aspect of all entities that constitute the universe*, and in their essence lies the source of creativity which is the ultimate characterization of reality.

Whitehead names these fundamental drops of experience that constitute reality *actual entities*, or *actual occasions*. These are not enduring substances but processes, or events, that continually generate and perish. All 'things' are essentially composed of these actual entities which then already involve a form of sentience, too basic to be called 'consciousness'. Nonetheless, as such, this process philosophy is a type of *panpsychism*, commonly called 'panexperientialism' with regard to Whitehead, as it is experience as opposed to consciousness that is ubiquitous. The direct seeds of this idea can be traced to William James and his substantiation of the panpsychist Gustav Fechner via Bergson,[4] but the origins of panpsychism can be witnessed in Schopenhauer, Leibniz, Spinoza, in Renaissance thinkers such as Bruno and Patrizi,[5] and within Ancient Greece.[6] The value of panpsychism lies in part in the fact that mind emerges not from matter, but is and always was a fundamental aspect of matter. It thereby overcomes the 'Hard Problem of Consciousness' (as coined by David Chalmers), the death knell of mechanism, by presenting consciousness as different in degree rather than in kind to the matter of physiology.

These actual entities are each a process of 'concrescence': of attaining valued self-existence out of the datum of the rest of the universe. This process of concrescence that creates an actual entity begins thus: an initial 'subjective aim' is provided to the actual entities which triggers the 'prehension' of the universe into a subjective form that comprises the mode of experience of the actual entity.

A subjective aim is a purpose, a *telos*,[7] that strives for self-existence and through that an aesthetic intensity of experience. It is provided by what

Whitehead calls the 'eternal urge of desire'[8], or 'God'. As this 'God' is more
idiosyncratically pantheistic, or panentheistic, than monotheistic, it is odd
that Whitehead did not rename this concept as well – a concept to which
we shall return. The initial subjective aim is provided by 'God', but the
subjective aim is then assimilated by the actual entity and becomes its own.[9]
Thus the actual entity becomes to this extent a *causa sui*.

The aim allows for the unity of experience that comprises the single actual
entity to derive in part from divergent data. As all existence is constituted by
actual entities, the experience here, the datum, is of other actual entities. The
reason Whitehead uses the term *'prehension' instead of 'perception'* is to
avoid the metaphysical stance that a representation is numerically distinct
from the object represented. This is the large error perpetrated by modern
philosophy and science, epitomized in the Kantian critique. In distinction to
this representationalist assumption, which only leads to solipsism, Whitehead
defines a 'prehension' as the *merging* of one experience – an actual entity –
into another actual entity. In other words, 'an actual entity is present in other
actual entities.'[10] This notion, named 'the principle of universal relativity',[11]
of prehension is analogous to the view of perception put forward by Henri
Bergson.[12] It can be said to be an anti-representationalist view of perception.
A part of the object becomes part of the subject, the implications of which
begin to efface the subject-object dichotomy that has so plagued modern
thought. Perception is not to be understood in the relation *appearance-to-
reality* but rather in the relation *part-to-whole*.

This fusion of other actual entities into a new unity include actual entities
of the immediate past and actual entities of the concurrent environment. The
novel actual entity thus inherits from its past experiences and forms of being,
but it is not entirely determined by them due to the subsequent subjective
aim. There is thus an identity and a contrast with its past that makes the
experience aesthetic because '[a]ll aesthetic experience is a feeling arising
out of the realization of contrast under identity.'[13] Whitehead identifies this
intrinsic aesthetic experience with the extrinsic physical principle that,

> *vibration enters into the ultimate nature of atomic
> organisms.*[14]

Thus,

> *physical vibrations are the expression among the
> abstractions of physical science of the fundamental
> principle of aesthetic experience.*[15]

Three points are to be noted here. The first is that Whitehead is implicitly employing a form of 'double-aspect theory', common amongst Idealists. Secondly, that this indicates the abstract, thus insufficient, ontology of science. Thirdly, that Whitehead identifies all decisive entities as organisms.

Regarding the first two points: that which 'science' considers to be matter is a presentation of something that already includes sentience. Thus matter is an abstraction from a larger reality, one of at least intrinsic sentience and extrinsic extension. To understand that nature has such an extrinsic and intrinsic reality is known as *double-aspect theory*, as opposed to a *single-aspect theory* that is the assumption of science.[16] Such a double-aspect view is encapsulated by the name of Arthur Schopenhauer's work, *The World as Will and Representation*. Both Schopenhauer and Whitehead saw that nature must be understood not only from without to within, but *vice versa*. In fact, Schopenhauer's passage on the matter is almost reflected in Whitehead:

> *We must learn to understand nature from ourselves, not ourselves from nature.*[17] – Schopenhauer

> *It is the accepted doctrine in physical science that a living body is to be interpreted according to what is known of other sections of the physical universe. This is a sound axiom, but it is double-edged. For it carries with it the converse deduction that other sections of the universe are to be interpreted in accordance with what we know of the human body.*[18] – Whitehead

This is an identity, but what contrasts the two thinkers is Schopenhauer's Representationalist view of perception rejected, as we have seen, in Whitehead. As such, it would be wrong to label Whitehead an *Idealist*.

With regard to the third point, Whitehead uses the term 'atomic organisms' because for him, and as cause of the name 'Philosophy of Organism', there is no absolute difference in kind between what is popularly named the 'organic' and 'inorganic'. *The line from animal, to organ, to cell, to molecule, to atom, to subatomic particle involves a difference of degree rather than a difference of kind.* It is but language based on unwitting metaphysics that has produced the (in)organic duality as a commonplace. Whitehead's philosophy is expressed succinctly by his declaration that,

Biology is the study of the larger organisms; whereas physics is the study of the smaller organisms.[19]

Let us return to the concrescent process that constitutes actual entities, and the prehensions that manifest their identity through fusion with other actual entities. *Whitehead names this immanent infusion of actual entities into one another their 'vector' character.* This vector character includes both 'positive' and 'negative prehensions'. A negative prehension is the enforced exclusion of certain actual entities into the new. This begins to create a certain perspective for the emerging actual entity. Positive prehensions can be further divided into 'physical prehensions' and 'conceptual prehensions' (also referred to as 'physical' and 'conceptual feelings').

A 'physical prehension' is one which prehends another actual entity. A 'conceptual prehension' is one which *only* prehends what is coined an 'eternal object', which for now we shall define loosely as *qualia*. A physical prehension objectifies in its own way another actual entity by means of the eternal objects it utilizes. In other words, an actual entity prehends another actual entity according to its own filtering system; thus actual entities differ in the way in which they experience the world. Analogously we might say that a bat and a cuttlefish view the same object in different ways according to their respective perceptual filtering systems. In actual entities, such a filtering system is called a 'subjective form', and is made up of the eternal objects that prehensions involve as the necessary means of their functioning, their becoming.

Therefore, through subjective form and negative prehensions guided by subjective aim, each actual entity is an experiential perspective on the universe. In this sense the philosophy is a *transNietzschean cosmological Perspectivism*. And this continual creation of new forms, ultimately unlimited, is Creativity itself: 'The creative action is the universe always becoming one in a particular unity of self-experience'.[20] This unity is akin in some respects to Leibniz's monadology, a similarity conducing Whitehead's synopsis of his own philosophy:

> *Each monadic creature is a mode of the process of "feeling" the world, of housing the world in one unit of complex feeling, in every way determinate. Such a unit is an "actual occasion"; it is the ultimate creature derivative from the creative process.*[21]

This process of feeling the world involves the 'ingression' of eternal objects into actual entities, an ingression that determines the actual entity. An eternal object is a mental quality, akin to the term 'quale', the singular of qualia – such phenomena as shades of colour and emotions. However, Whitehead makes eternal objects synonymous with the phrase 'pure potentials of the universe',[22] thereby placing them in contradistinction to actuality. The eternal objects thus subsist within a transcendent realm, yet always ingress into actuality and so become the ongoing advance into novelty. There is a public nod to Plato's theory of Forms or Ideas (*Eidos*), and Aristotle's 'universals', but these terms are avoided again due to their metaphysical connotations that are incompatible with the Philosophy of Organism.

In a physical prehension (actual entity to actual entity), eternal objects act as mediators determining the subjective form of the former entity for the latter. In all cases, this really involves a myriad of actual entities streaming into the new one. Initially, these incoming actual entities are prehended conformally, that is, the antecedent actual entities bequeath their own eternal objects to the newborn. This initial relational phase maintains 'the solidarity of the universe'[23] as the present inherits the past and by so doing ensures regularities and endurances of nature. It is notable here that this vector transition is the immanent experience of causality – named the 'presentational mode of causal efficacy' in higher grades of organism – and as such presents a refutation of Hume's claim that causality is not experienced. *To an extent this, along with the rejection of representationalism, renders Kant's critical philosophy redundant.*

This conformal inheritance of eternal objects is commonly known as efficient causation in its abstracted extrinsic aspect (i.e. for mechanism), and in this abstraction is the transmission of a form of energy. The supplemental phase of eternal objects in an actual entity is one of immanent final causation, teleology. The actual entity, having received conformal eternal objects now has a 'decision'[24] to employ further eternal objects to realize its subjective aim. These supplemental eternal objects constitute the actual entity's determination as a unique subject through its subjective form. As stated, the initial aim is provided by God, but the supplemental subjective aim is determined by the entity itself. This is what ultimately conditions the creativity of reality. The subjective aim is to reach the experiential intensity of 'satisfaction' – actually felt by 'God', as we shall divine.

Once an actual entity has reached satisfaction, which is a generic term[25] and so not indicative of a single type of experience, it transforms from a subject into a 'superject', meaning that it is no longer an active process but the datum for the next actual entity, *ad infinitum*. The completed actual entity passes into 'objective immortality', that is, the existent past that informs the present, and it is this that pushes creativity: 'the birth of a new instance is the passage into novelty.'[26]

An actual entity is an event which in its abstracted individuality is on the micro scale. On the relative macro scale in which we humans abide, we prehend actual entities in 'nexūs', in aggregates. When a nexus (singular) has a defining characteristic throughout its members, Whitehead calls it a 'society'. This characteristic maintains the society as an enduring object because the characteristic is transmitted both temporally and spatially throughout the society. An electron is an example of a society for Whitehead[27], which has its charged characteristic amongst others. Societies exist within societies, loosely illustratable as a concentric circle with actual entities assuming the centre. The outer societies influence the inner ones, and *vice versa*, and so the actual entity at the heart would have a different essence were it not within that particular society. An electron can exist within the society of the atom, that of the molecule, that of the cell, that of the organism, of the planet, of the galaxy, of the universe at present, and that still as within the society of electromagnetism, further still within the 'society of pure extension'[28] – that is, within the universe as extended spatially in three dimensions. This cosmological social hierarchy is inherently mutually influential and thus stable, but ultimately even the outer rings are not eternal:

> our spatio-physical epoch will pass into the background
> of the past.[29]

Just as the molecules within one's body act differently according to their subordination within the human system, so it is on a cosmic scale:

> The molecules within an animal body exhibit certain
> peculiarities of behaviour not to be detected outside an
> animal body. In fact, living societies [organisms] illustrate
> the doctrine that the laws of nature develop together with
> the societies which constitute an epoch.[30]

Humans are personal types of *'living societies', which is Whitehead's term for what is traditionally labeled 'organisms'*. One must recall that for Whitehead's philosophy, all entities are organisms with experience. Very complex organisms are thus distinguished as 'living', and this includes single-celled creatures. Whitehead continues to define a living society as one which has a 'reaction adapted to the capture of [experiential] intensity, under a large variety of circumstances.' In other words, living societies are structures that in their complex autopoiesis (high degree of self-sufficiency) allow for more intensive feelings than lesser societies and entities could allow.

Complex living societies prehend nexūs by the process of 'transmutation' – that is, the process whereby the actual entities are prehended as macrocosmic wholes rather than as a plurality. These transmuted feelings begin the approach to abstraction that is constitutive of consciousness (and the errors of thought): transmutation eliminates detail. Our human experience is as that of an actual entity, but our initial datum is microcosmic data transmuted into one. We living societies are flooded with the data of our individual cells, which themselves are flooded by data from their environment (both physiological and external thereto). In the more complex living societies this flood is narrowed into a centrality of control, and the 'organ of central control of very high-grade character is the brain'.[31] *Note here that the brain is the organ of central control; it is not the organ productive of sentience.* It streamlines multiple sentiences rather than produces sentience *per se*. A 'living person' (a 'soul') – not of necessity human – is a living society which intakes multiple data from the past and from the environmental present, and to its extent of power is regnant there over. Whitehead compares a human to an autocracy in this respect; a plant to a democracy. Sometimes the centrifugal control lapses and we experience such things as multiple-personality disorder ('[which] in primitive times has been interpreted as demoniac possession'[32]), and even, Whitehead claims, the direct aspects of other complex living societies. Against the 'Problem of Other Minds', Whitehead writes:

> *we must also allow for the possibility that we can detect in ourselves direct aspects of the mentalities of higher organisms. The claim that the cognition of alien mentalities must necessarily be by means of indirect inferences from aspects of shape and of sense-objects is wholly unwarranted by this philosophy of organism. The fundamental principle is that whatever merges into actuality, implants its aspects in every individual event.*[33]

Associated with the transmuted feelings of living societies are the complex eternal objects. These are similar to the 'complex ideas' of Locke and Hume, and range after the 'group g' of the simple eternal objects of actual entities to the 'vertex' which is the sole maximally complex eternal object of any finite set of combinations.[34] Humans are superior in having the possibility of ingression of the eternal objects inclusive of the vertex; but, in conformity with his panpsychism, Whitehead reminds us that,

> the emotional appetitive elements in our conscious experience are those which most closely resemble the basic elements of all physical experience.[35]

Here again we can note a similarity with Schopenhauer and his fundamental 'will' (*Wille*) that is both experienced by man and by the forces of the cosmos. Nietzsche's advance of Schopenhauer, with his 'will to power' perhaps reaches closer proximity to Whitehead when we consider the latter's view of 'a bewildering complexity of such societies, favouring each other, competing with each other',[36] and his claim that 'the societies which [the living society] destroys are its food. This food is destroyed by dissolving it into somewhat simpler social elements ... this interplay takes on the form of robbery ... life is robbery'.[37]

Unlike Nietzsche, however, Whitehead involves God in his philosophy. Yet, we should not identify this deity with that of the Abrahamic religions with Whom Nietzsche concerned himself. In fact, contrary to the Christianesque tinge of the 'Process Theology' which Whitehead's thought instigated, the god found in Whitehead is more pagan:

> [The] function of God is analogous to the remorseless working of things in Greek and Buddhist thought ... the ruthlessness of God can be personified as Atè, the goddess of mischief.[38]

Atè, also spelt Äte, is depicted in Homer[39] as the daughter of Zeus. In her mischief she presents resemblance to the characterization of the Nordic god Loki, father of Hel, of the giant wolf Fenrir, and of the sea serpent Ormr that surrounds the worlds of the Nordic cosmology, biting its own tail – thus being an instantiation of the universal ouroboros symbol. In connection to Nietzsche the ouroboros symbolizes the 'Eternal Return'; in the Nordic case the serpent will let go (signifying the destruction of the epoch), fittingly thereby denoting novelty in Whitehead's sense rather than the circularity in Nietzsche's.[40] *Hel* is both a goddess and the underworld realm over which she reigns. In Shakespeare's *Julius Caesar*, the Bard connects the Greek goddess with the dark underworld:

And Caesar's spirit, ranging for revenge,
With Atë by his side come hot from Hell,
Shall in these confines with a monarch's voice
Cry "Havoc!" and let slip the dogs of war ...[41]

The reason for this poetic ingression is chiefly to emphasize the darker nihilistic aspects of the god of Whom Whitehead speaks, to bond this representation with shadowy facets of psy-phen, and to distance Him (Her) from the rather mawkish idolatry (S)He receives in much process discussion. It is no exaggeration: Whitehead himself employs dark poetry against the Semitic theory of a wholly transcendent God. Opposing that Semitic deity to Plato's contrary in his *Timaeus*, Whitehead quotes from Milton's *Paradise Lost* on the journey of Satan across Chaos:

The secrets of the hoary Deep – a dark
Illimitable ocean, without bound,
Without dimension; where length, breadth, and height,
And time, and place, are lost; where eldest Night
And Chaos, ancestors of Nature, hold
Eternal anarchy, amidst the noise
Of endless wars, and by confusion stand.[42]

Whitehead immediately thereafter identifies Satan (equated with Loki[43]) with the God of his philosophy:

Satan's journey helped to evolve order; for he left a
permanent track, useful for the devils and the damned.[44]

Furthermore, the panpsychism of the philosophy of organism is more inclined towards the worship of nature and nature spirits which exist in the animism of non-Christianized pagan cultures. Further still, the universal immanence of God is more akin to Eastern varieties of religion. It is a pantheism qualified as panentheism due to the eternal objects which in their potentiality still subsist transcendentally. But, though God, actual entities and creativity comprise the ultimate notions of the philosophy, Whitehead rejects any dogma regarding the definite nature of deity:

as to the nature of God[, t]here is nothing here in the nature
of proof ... and the system is confessedly inadequate. The

*deductions from it in this particular sphere of thought
cannot be looked upon as more than suggestions.*[45]

But let us begin the revelation according to Whitehead. God has two
natures: the 'primordial' and the 'consequent'. One could say that these are
akin respectively to the traditional theological characterizations of God as
transcendent and immanent.

The 'Primordial Nature of God' is the realm of eternal objects. These are
potentials not actuals and so only subsist in God's mind until they are ingressed
into actual entities and their societies. This is a realm of every potential
actuality, of infinite extent. It is every quale that could be instantiated, beyond
the common imaginations of us mere human mortals. If this infinity of eternal
objects were nonexistent, the universe could not progress and would eternally
recur the same experiential and physical phenomena that were inherited from
the past. Without eternal objects, Whitehead argues, there would be but a
static universe without complexity. Novel qualia of the future do not actually
exist, but must potentially exist in order to fuel this progression of complexity
that we can witness. They cannot exist latently in actual non-experiential
matter, as such matter is not productive of qualia, but an abstraction derived
from qualia. The question becomes then their ontological status: how do they
exist if not actually? They exist potentially, they 'subsist' (as Whitehead's
student and colleague Bertrand Russell said of Universals[46]). This subsistence
of a plurality of potentials can be given a name – Whitehead names it 'God'
with reference to His primordial nature.

The primordial nature of God, in itself, i.e. in abstraction (from His
consequent nature), is not conscious: '[when we] consider God in the
abstraction of a primordial actuality, we must ascribe to him neither fullness
of feeling, nor consciousness.'[47] This is because consciousness, the crown of
experience, is for Whitehead the *feeling* of a contrast between fact (objectified
actual entities) and potentiality (eternal objects), which is thus not an operation
attainable by the latter realm of the eternal objects themselves, i.e. God's
primordial nature. Rather, God's primordial role is as the 'lure for feeling,
the eternal urge of desire',[48] this (S)He does by bestowing the initial phase of
each actual entity's subjective aim (His 'transcendent decision'[49]), and then
by providing relevant eternal objects for the entity's subsequent 'immanent
decision'.[50] God in this way is a final cause of the activity of the universe:
the initial subjective aim from God is a divine element of teleology in nature,
explicitly echoing Aristotle's Prime Mover that so influenced Christianity via
St Thomas Aquinas. But the supplemental decision is a secular teleology:
God and creature alike have their own purposes.

'The "Consequent Nature of God" is the physical prehension by God of the actualities of the evolving universe.'[51] *That is to say, God in His 'consequent' nature is the total multiple consciousnesses and feelings of each actual entity and society in the universe.* 'He shares with every new creation its actual world; and the concrescent creature is objectified in God as a novel element in God's objectification of that actual world'.[52] God's incursion into actual experiences is God's desire:

> *God's purpose in the creative advance is the evocation of intensities. The evocation of societies is purely subsidiary to this absolute end.*[53]

God thus conditions each act of creation and participates in its individual sentient intensity. He is as a dipolar deity both creator and created, the artist who paints Himself into actual existence. God as such is Himself an everlasting actual entity, a process Himself, and in the philosophy of organism is second to Creativity in terms of the fundamental principles of reality. God is the clockwork by which Creativity unwinds its infinite coil. Furthermore, in accord with Gustav Fechner's pansycho-pantheism,[54]

> *God is that function in the world by reason of which our purposes are directed to ends which in our own consciousness are impartial as to our own interests. ... The consciousness which is individual in us, is universal in him.*[55]

If we ascribe sentience to a cell within our body, it would be oblivious to our overarching personal aims. Yet those aims, those final causes, would involve the transmutation of a plurality of such cellular sentiences into our unified consciousness, and we, as a whole, could direct the activity, and thus experience, unwittingly, of the cell by, say, our decision to move.[56] Likewise, with God and His body: the universe. We are the cells, He is the body – both of which are mutually influential. Therefore the 'God' of Whom we speak is neither omnipotent nor omniscient, considering in the latter respect the uncreated hence unknowable future. Thus the word 'God' is hardly appropriate, and we can still maintain with Nietzsche that *Gott ist tot* if we concede that Whitehead commits a *death by a thousand qualifications*.

Even God's omnibenevolence is questionable due to Whitehead's claim that he 'finds the foundation of the world in the aesthetic experience ... [and so] [a]ll order is therefore aesthetic order, and the moral order is merely certain aspects of aesthetic order'.[57] There may be very many competing moral orders all of which exhibit an aesthetic quality in terms of their harmony. Further, *Whitehead's moral relativism, which is a result of subordinating morality to aesthetics*, can be garnered when we read that '[t]he terms morality, logic, religion, art, have each of them been claimed as exhausting the whole meaning of importance. Each of them denotes a subordinate species. But the genus stretches beyond any finite group of species'.[58] If the alleged laws of nature are in flux, the laws of morality would analogously suffer the same, if more frequent, fate. But to be explicit in his nihilism, Whitehead writes:

> *There is no one behaviour system belonging to the essential character of the universe, as the universal moral ideal ... Thus morality does not indicate what you are to do in mythological abstractions. It does concern the general ideal which should be the justification for any particular objective. The destruction of man, or of an insect, or of a tree, or of the Parthenon, may be moral or immoral.*[59]

Whitehead's 'God' is in fact the devil. For Whitehead the world is in flux, and so moral systems are as well. A moral ideology is itself a society which influences its members, and, as history shows, is something that itself generates and degenerates. Nothing actual is stable, morality included. Moralities are belief systems that instantiate intensities of emotion but cannot substantiate their absolute objectivity. Dionysus would be a more suitable icon for Whitehead's desirous deity, and again we breach into the Nietzschean immoralist realm. 'Have I been understood? – Dionysus against the Crucified',[60] exclaims Nietzsche in the last sentence of his autobiography. With respect to psy-phen, Whitehead's God is more likened still to Dionysus' epithet Iacchus, god of the Eleusinian Mysteries. Whichever icon one uses, Whitehead's position on the deiform entity is open-ended:

> *What further can be known about God must be sought in the region of particular experiences, and therefore rests on an empirical basis.*[61]

To these regions we shall now travel following our summary of the philosophy of organism.

Mechanism is an abstract cosmology that as such reaches a terminus of problems. In its stead, Whitehead offers a creative cosmology. Creativity is inaugurated by the bequeathing of an initial subjective aim by God to what thenceforth becomes a subject, a monad. By this initial aim the subject, an actual entity, prehends the incoming data of its environment. Particular data actually become part of the subject via positive and negative prehensions. These prehensions take on a subjective form conditioned by the eternal objects which God provides through His primordial nature. The subsequent subjective aim of the actual entity decides upon a suitable means of prehending, thus reacting to, its environment for the ultimate end of attaining aesthetic satisfaction: an intense feeling that completes the concrescence of the actual entity. God in His consequent nature experiences this satisfaction and the subjective forms thereto; it is His own desire to do so. He thus provides the condition for the desires in the universe and is Himself conditioned by the satisfaction of these desires. Subsequently the actual entity perishes as an active process but gains objective immortality as data for the proceeding actual entities. Actual entities are sentient in a non-conscious manner, and so the philosophy is a form of panpsychism: where mind is ubiquitous. Matter-energy is merely the abstracted extrinsic appearance of this inner mentality. Actual entities can aggregate into societies, which are named thus because the members share a characteristic that mutually influences the whole. Living societies include animals, and these permit the transmutation of the myriad feelings that are the actual entities into complex eternal objects. God's aim is to partake of these intense complex actualized eternal objects, a participation that enriches His divine quality. Thus God is an actual entity that acts as a conduit for the flow of creativity according to His aesthetic final causes. *There is no stability, no substance, in the actual universe – everything is a process, a downpour of drops and splashes of experience.*

Psy-phen and the Philosophy of Organism

Physical wandering is still important [for mankind's evolution], but greater still is the power of man's spiritual adventures – adventures of thought, adventures of passionate feeling, adventures of aesthetic experience.[62]

Assuming Whitehead's cosmology, it would seem difficult to deny that psychedelic experience would be the greatest means by which God's aesthetic adventures of growth could be attained. *A God who desired intense, complex actualized peaks of experience would strive to proliferate psy-phen: the vertexes of sentience.*

The interpretation of psy-phen under the philosophy of organism shall thence be examined via this path: *we shall overview the physical, chemical, initiations and reverberations and then their mental pole. This pole will consider the notion of psy-phen as immersion into God (or, Devil): from both His primordial and consequent nature. Thereafter we shall be led to consider further types of immersion.*

We begin from the physical. The ingestion of psychedelic molecules flood the body, trespass via the blood-brain barrier into the cerebral matter, and essentially clog the synapses. The molecules of common serotonergic psychedelics – such as psilocybin, mescaline, LSD and DMT – interact with the serotonin receptors within the synapse due to their structural similarity to the endogenous serotonin molecule. The normal bodily functioning of input and output is thereby severely disturbed. The brain's role as the 'organ of central control',[63] founders as such. Incoming data for transmutation is fractured and so inefficiently reciprocated. Thus, control over bodily movement becomes impaired, relative to factors such as psychedelic type, dose, digestive status, body mass and type, antecedent mind set, and so on – a commonly experienced cloddishness ranging to physical incapacity.

In this year of writing, 2015, the precise neural activity correlative of psy-phen is in its infancy, as neuroscience itself is, from a long-term perspective. It would be easy to believe that the understanding of psy-phen will be gained once this neuroscientific project has been completed. This however, will not be the case: a full neuroscientific knowledge would not sufficiently explain consciousness, let alone the vertex of consciousness, psy-phen. *Knowing the complex activity of matter-energy, in this case the activity of physiology in terms of patterns of synchronicity and so forth, is not identical to knowing the correlative activity of sentience. This is because matter-energy is an abstraction from the total actuality which already includes sentience. Considering this abstraction as a reality, as mechanism does, is to commit an example of what Whitehead calls* the fallacy of misplaced concreteness. *This fallacy is thus the germ of the Hard Problem of Consciousness, as well as many other problems such as the rejection of teleology which results in the paradoxical inefficacy of reason.*[64] Furthermore, neuroscience concerns itself with mammalian brains. But if we consider beings such as the octopus, we realize that their intelligent behaviour is indicative of a complex consciousness, and yet their brains radically differ from those of mammals. Two-thirds of an octopus' brain lie within its arms, for instance. Even were we to fully understand the operations of this eight-armed neurology, we would not thereby fully understand the consciousness of the creature. Likewise with psy-phen, a potential full knowledge of its correlated physiological activity will not be sufficient knowledge, though it is indubitably interesting and medically important. Consciousness overflows the anthropocentric remit of neuroscience. If we consider reality in its concrete, non-abstracted, form – as Whitehead presents his über-empiricism – we attain deeper metaphysical insights.

After psychedelic intake, mental activity, concurrent to common behavioural inactivity, mushrooms. The multitudinous literature of 'trip reports' offer glimpses of that mental height to the uninitiated. But in analogy with neuroscience-to-consciousness, literature-to-psy-phen exposes a chasm that cannot be bridged from one side alone. Psy-phen can be, in accord with William James' categorization of mystical experiences,[65] ineffable. The imagery and feelings one meets make even these two concepts incompetent of description. However, there exists still a qualitative scale of reports; amongst the best one must include Thomas De Quincey, Henri Michaux and Aldous Huxley. Huxley invokes Bergson for explanatory purposes, and Bergson himself wrote to William James of a dream experience that reads very much like an instance of psy-phen, especially of the DMT variety:

> *I believed myself to be to be present before a superb spectacle – generally the sight of a landscape of intense colours, through which I was travelling at high speed and which gave me such a profound impression of reality that I could not believe, during the first moments of waking up, that it was a simple dream.*[66]

There are some indications that DMT is produced endogenously,[67] a possibility which could explain this particular similarity of dream and psy-phen – though the latter is mostly far more potent. Bergson suggests here a veridical aspect of his experience, and in fact encourages James to continue his explorations in this respect: 'How I would like you to pursue this study of "the noetic value of abnormal mental states"!'[68] We shall return to the value of psy-phen, but let us first attempt to generalize its character.

It is useful to divide psy-phen into sensorially-open and sensorially-closed modes. This is certainly not absolute as the senses will always have some affect upon the person under influence. But there is a marked distinction between the psy-phen of open-eyed observation of the external environment, and closed-eyed observation of the internal environment. Psy-phen is highly eclectic, but can at least be distinguished as non-ordinary human sentience. Further details shall be presented throughout the following investigation.

Psy-phen can be interpreted as an immersion into 'God', as here understood. God ordinarily immerses Himself into us as He is the combined actual multiplicity of the universe of which we are a part; our individual perspectives are His partial perspectives. I am sound, you are vision, He is both and more in one. With psy-phen we reverse that immersion: we diffuse into Him rather than He into us. But further, by so doing, we enrich both parties because God requires us actualities to reap actual consciousness of what in Him is merely potential (the eternal objects). As mentioned, the primordial nature of God which is the realm of eternal objects is not conscious. We shall examine the relation of psy-phen to the primordial nature of God (PNG), and then the relation to the consequent nature of God (CNG).

The PNG is the dimension of pure potentiality. It is infinite in terms of the plurality of eternal objects, arranged in hierarchies of complexity and chiefly divided into subjective and objective forms, e.g. emotions and numbers, respectively. In an actuality such as we, in our non-psychedelic state, we initially receive eternal objects that conform to the immediate past and the immediate surroundings. That is thereafter supplemented by a phase of ingression of eternal objects of partly our own decision though also determined by the principle of relativity, i.e. the vectoring in of other objective entities. Negative prehensions exclude the majority of eternal objects into us. This is in line with Nietzsche and Bergson's view that we only perceive that which is of practical use, that which can potentially aid our development, our power over the environment. Our human geometric mode of abstract perception is only possible due to this limitation – as Bergson writes:

> *The distinct outlines which we see in an object, and which give it its individuality, are only the design of a certain kind of influence that we might exert on a certain point of space: it is the plan of our eventual actions ... Suppress this action, and with it consequently those main directions which by perception are traced out for it in the entanglement of the real, and the individuality of the body is re-absorbed in the universal interaction which, without doubt, is reality itself.*[69]

We do not prehend, at least not in the 'perceptual mode of presentational immediacy',[70] *the vast welter of energy of electromagnetic and other varieties, but only those slits of potential energy-experience that serve our practical needs.* These needs are centrally co-ordinated by the brain. Hence, when the brain's practical functioning has been disturbed by those chemicals that can breach the blood-brain barrier to do so, and moreover jigsaw into the existing structures of that brain, the central authority of the person no longer exists to decide upon exclusion through negative prehensions. Thus descend like the falling angels from the heavens the eternal objects from God's primordial realm. They now bear little if any conformation to the actual environment. In the aforementioned sensorially-closed world of psy-phen, there is accordingly even less conformity. *We thus close our eyes to see.* The primordial nature of God is prehended, without conformity and hence with an arbitrary style. In this sense, the modern term for psychedelic, *entheogen* seems apt as it means 'generating the divine within'. *However, as this is only one aspect of psy-phen, it is in fact an inappropriate term; the word* psychedelic *is more neutral as it avoids an explanatory connotation of its experience, and is less limiting.*

We are not becoming God, we are vectoring into Him, fusing with Him to an extent greater than the common fusion thereto with its proliferative negative prehensions. It is an apotheosis qualified by symbiosis. God benefits by this reversed infusion because the potential becomes actual (though not physical) through our part, and hence conscious. PNG is unconscious; psy-phen, conscious. By entering PNG via psy-phen, the CNG is activated and supremely enriched, as are we. The creator and the created fuse to attain experiences transcending practical precedents. *Psy-phen can offer levels of aesthetic appreciation transcendent, that is beyond the scope of evolutionarily-produced practically attuned minds. Such aesthetic immersion is truly of immense value to God and man.* Whitehead suggests that,

> *Human beings require something which absorbs them for a time, something out of the routine which they can stare at. ... [G]reat art is more than a transient refreshment. It is something which adds to the permanent richness of the soul's self-attainment. ... It transforms the soul into the permanent realization of values extending beyond its former self. ... In regard to the aesthetic needs of civilized society the reactions of science have been unfortunate. Its materialistic basis has directed attention to things as opposed to values.*[71]

Psy-phen enriches us, and it enriches God as his purpose is the evocation of experiential intensities through His creatures. *It would seem that psychedelics are divine sacraments the use of which most effectively fulfill the divine purpose. In this sense, their prohibition can be looked upon as a cardinal sin.* A new sin to match a new God. Again, we do not mean God when we say God. God's definition is in flux, and His essence may very well be cognized more purely in psy-phen, as is analogously claimed by the Mystics – yet even His essence in its consequent nature is subject to flux.

The ultra-magnificence of sensorially-closed psy-phen far supercedes that of imagination, and thereby falsifies the traditional empiricist claim that all ideas are faint copies of impressions. *Psy-phen falsifies Hume's claim* that,

> *though our thought seems to possess this unbounded liberty, we shall find, upon a nearer examination, that it is really confined within very narrow limits, and that all this creative power of the mind amounts to no more than the faculty of compounding, transposing, augmenting, or diminishing the materials afforded us by the senses and experience [feelings].*[72]

Psy-phen can present to us novelties, not combined actualities of the past. We are apprehending the delimited potentials of cognition. In entering the mind of 'God' in this way, we access the infinite bank of possibility that conditions the advance of creativity in the universe. *The common ineffability of these experiences indicate their novelty: words are not created for phenomena that are never considered.*

Through psychedelic intake we have modified our brain and body and *temporarily wrought divine anarchy upon the ordinary autocracy directing our cognition and behaviour*, a break down of what Leibniz would call the 'dominant monad'. It is this sovereign who directs decisions regarding the inclusion or exclusion of eternal objects according to their use to the body. The take down of this dominant monad, this sovereign will to power, via psychedelics would entail both the inclusion of bodily irrelevant eternal objects and the effacing of the apperception of that dictator, that ego. This autocrat is vital for the organism in general though – Whitehead writes, 'Any tendency to a high-grade multiple personality would be self-destructive by the antagonism of divergent aims. In other words, such multiple personality is destructive of the very essence of life, which is conformation of purpose.'[73] And indeed we find that so-called 'ego-loss' is amongst the most commonly expressed aspects of psy-phen. Furthermore, without the dominant monad extracting bodily use from its surroundings, more focus can be directed to the aesthetic side of perception. Separation from the will was for Schopenhauer the means to the pure appreciation of beauty, a talent reserved for the genius:

> *genius is the ability to leave entirely out of sight our own interest, our willing, and our aims, and consequently to discard entirely our own personality for a time, in order to remain pure knowing subject, the clear eye of the world ... Imagination has been rightly recognized as an essential element of genius.*[74]

Psy-phen offers a moment of genius to all, an imagination unfettered by the body's practical will, its 'ego'. This is not to say that psy-phen cannot be later used for the 'ego', a most natural facet of our nature and of nature as a whole – a fact overlooked by much psychedelic literature. The 'ego', or the will, serves to push the evolution of life into the complex forms that provide greater value in the universe. Pride could be no sin for Whitehead's God. To judge the ego as immoral is to judge nature Herself by employing the belief in a static objective morality; the very judgement itself is a method of the ego. For Nietzsche, the 'ego' is a transmutation of the will to power which is the fundamental inner pathos and drive of all energy; it is akin to the immanent subjective aim of Whitehead's actual entities. Nietzsche writes,

> *The victorious concept "force" ... still needs to be completed: an inner will must be ascribed to it, which I designate as "will to power," i.e., as an insatiable desire to manifest power; or as the employment and exercise of power, as a creative drive ... one is obliged to understand all motion, all "appearances," all "laws," only as symptoms of an inner event.*[75]

For Nietzsche, as in Leibniz and Whitehead, there is a hierarchy of wills within an organism. Psy-phen subdues the leviathan thereby unleashing chaos. The body loses that overall self-interest which guides perception but thereby gains interest in the non-self. As Aldous Huxley relates,

> *though perception is enormously improved, the will suffers a profound change for the worse. The mescalin taker sees*

no reason for doing anything in particular and finds most
of the causes for which, at ordinary times, he was prepared
to act and suffer, profoundly uninteresting. He can't be
bothered with them, for the good reason that he has better
things to think about.[76]

This shattering of the sense of the sovereign self, this 'ego-loss' is not by that fact a leap into the unified mind of God. Loss of self could initiate an upward or downward incursion. Upward incursion would mean entry into the mind of God in the sense of PNG incursion, as discussed, or in the sense of entry into the unified consciousness of God. This would be a prehension of unity with the rest of nature that is His pantheistic temporal essence. Such empathy is again rather common in the literature, and common in certain types of religious experience. It is the 'perennial philosophy' spoken of by Aldous Huxley, and akin to the henology[77] of Plotinus. William James writes that,

we finite minds may simultaneously be co-conscious
with one another in a superhuman intelligence ... there
are religious experiences of a specific nature ... [that]
point with reasonable probability to the continuity of our
consciousness with a wider spiritual environment from
which the ordinary prudential man ... is shut off.[78]

I classify psy-phen as a type of religious experience, regardless of the veridicality or not thereof. It is not an unusual equation when one considers that James goes so far as to state that even the 'drunken consciousness is one bit of the mystic consciousness'.[79] If that be one bit, then highly dosed psy-phen would be the whole bottle.

Such entry into the mind of God may even separate a subject from mutual vectorisation to complete subsequent identification. Despite calling Descartes' Substance Dualism a disaster for European thought,[80] Whitehead speculates that,

The everlasting nature of God, which in a sense is
non-temporal and in another sense is temporal may
establish with the soul [personal society] a peculiarly
intense relationship of mutual immanence. Thus in some
important sense the existence of the soul may be freed from
its complete dependence upon the bodily organization.[81]

The psychedelic shattering of the sovereign self can also lead to a downward incursion. One is reminded that the 'claim that the cognition of alien mentalities must necessarily be by means of indirect inferences from aspects of shape and of sense-objects is wholly unwarranted by this philosophy of organism'.[82] Whitehead's philosophy involves the vector factor of experience: the prehension of an organism or society thereof actually *is* a part of that entity within us. When one further considers that the 'physical' aspect of prehension – e.g. the electromagnetic vibrations of colour – contains an intrinsic mental aspect (experience), one realizes that such vectoring includes the feelings of another as part of oneself. Whitehead after all calls these prehensions 'physical feelings' (as opposed to the 'conceptual feelings' of eternal objects alone). Our personal feelings are the transmuted multiple feelings of our bodily cells, whose experience has further been inherited from the body's environment, i.e. other organisms (in nexūs). The transmutation is controlled by the central authority of the body: the brain. Now, as psychedelics inhibit the normal functioning of the brain and body, the multitudinous feelings of the cells are no longer unified. *Thus it is feasible that in certain cases psy-phen allows identification with the experiential world of a cell – one becomes the cell.* Its feelings would be so alien as to make it completely indescribable and incomprehensible to ordinary human consciousness. One can only speculate that the sometimes utterly alien aspects of psy-phen in the sensorially-closed mode could be the experience of such downward incursion. Furthermore, when we consider the likelihood that other organisms experience time at different durations to humans relative to objective events, the common distortion of time reported in psy-phen is set in an explanatory framework. A cell may experience the duration of our standard second as we do a minute, hour, day, week, and so on. A molecule, also organic and sentient in the philosophy of organism, would have a relative phenomenal duration different once more.

When further considered in the sensorially-open mode, we would consider intra-organic vectorisation to be horizontal rather than vertical. Consider this report from Paul Devereaux:

> *[On LSD] I found my awareness slipping inside that of the daffodil. While still being conscious of sitting in a chair, I could also sense my petals! Then an exquisite sensation cascaded through me, and I knew I was experiencing light falling on those petals. It was virtually orgasmic, the haptic equivalent of an angelic choir ... A mythic atmosphere hung like the most delicate gossamer in the air.*[83]

With the practical will dissolved, negative prehensions concerned with maintenance and development of the body erode away. In their place, more positive prehensions flood in and what was before viewed a mundane flower becomes a temple of intense complex beauty and sublimity. This increased aesthetic interest is a commonality in psy-phen, enriching people's subsequent lives with its lasting appeal. We prehend more of the same object, we thus become more of the same object. It appears that this identity can become near total, and so the majority of our feelings become those of the object, which, in panpsychism, always themselves include sentience if the objects are autopoietic.

Bergson argues for the possibility of such intra-organic vectorisation by juxtaposing intellect and intuition, where intellect is the cognition of outer representations and intuition the empathy of inner feelings:

> *intuition may bring the intellect to recognize that life does not quite go into the category of the many nor yet into that of the one[;] ... by the sympathetic communication which [intuition] establishes between us and the rest of the living, by the expansion of our consciousness which brings it about, it introduces us into life's domain, which is reciprocal interpenetration, endlessly continued creation.*[84]

By enabling such intra-organic 'sympathy', the CNG is enriched: the novel experience of the prehended external organism is complemented by its comparison to and integration with standard human experience, thus a new vertex is realized in actuality. Moreover, by allowing such high-grade vectorisation, psy-phen consoles Bergson's grievance that,

> *Consciousness, in man, is pre-eminently intellect. It might have been, it ought, so it seems, to have been also intuition ... A complete and perfect humanity would be that in which these two forms of conscious activity should attain their full development.*[85]

Psy-phen completes humanity by offering balance to our over-intellectualisation that favours the shell over the emerging life-form within, the abstract over the experienced, the dead over the living.

Yet, the claim is not being made that all psy-phen is of novelty. There is a relation to personal memory in the psychedelic experience which can often take a central role. Thus it would be an error to claim that psy-phen was either purely divine, entheogenic, or intra-organic. The mnemonic aspect may offer therapeutic assistance to those with burdensome and perhaps suppressed histories. Like Bergson, the past for Whitehead is immortal: all that has happened still exists in the entities that continue to inform the present. In fact, immediate memory vectoring into the new occasion is causality, experienced from within. An actual entity is constituted in part by its predecessors and in turn partly constitutes the new by way of objective immortality. Even in this non-divine mnemonic psy-phen, the experience can be profound. Thomas De Quincey notes such an occasion during his opium-induced psy-phen:

> *The minutest incidents of childhood, or forgotten scenes*
> *of later years, were often revived ... placed as they were*
> *before me, in dreams like intuitions, and clothed in all their*
> *evanescent circumstances and accompanying feelings,*
> *I recognized them instantaneously. ... I feel assured,*
> *that there is no such thing as forgetting[;] traces once*
> *impressed upon the memory are indestructible.*[86]

The past exists in the ever-increasing present, but its influence is conditioned by concurrent concerns, most of which entail the negative prehensions of those past occasions of little or no relevance to the present. When the autocratic self loses power, those past occasions gain a foothold in consciousness. When we are asleep, without immediate present sensory concerns, the past can creep up into conscious light once more. In a like fashion, psy-phen as physiological anarchist offers the same access. To the accusation that such vivid recall as De Quincey's are 'false memories', one replies that such phenomena are either recollections of former imaginations, or imaginations believed to be of former occasions. Either way, such 'false memories' are not inconsistent with the profound true memories described.

Hence, psy-phen allows far less limited access to both eternal objects that have been experienced in the past and those that are new in the ingression (physical and conceptual feelings). *Memory and novel phenomenology are both included and often intertwined.* We thus may experience a familiar place that suddenly takes on a novel aspect. We may then open our eyes and be waylaid the beauty of a table leg or daffodil.

We may then sensorially close and meet Äte, our God Who is in this case both object and subject: God is attaining heights Herself through us. *When we experience psychedelics, God experiences psychedelics; and due to our*

upward incursion into Her more extensive unconscious primordial nature,
she becomes self-conscious through Her conscious consequent nature. Psy-
phen allows the CNG to access the PNG. Psychedelics allow God to become
self-conscious.

In sum, psychedelics assail the brain thereby effacing the autocrat who
ordinarily conditions our survival and development. Sentience is then
fractured and open to a variety of paths. There is the upward incursion into
the primordial nature of God wherein we find the infinity of eternal objects,
here prehended purely, without concern for one's body. There is a downward
incursion into the subordinate societies within the body with their foreign
forms of sentience. There is the horizontal incursion into external organisms,
the intra-organic vectorisation that offers alien forms of sentience. Rendering
incursion three-dimensional, we can say that psy-phen also offers backwards
incursion into the past, memories otherwise long lost. Whether there is a
forward incursion, and further dimensions, I shall leave to the psychonaut
to explore. The three dimensions of incursion here identified are moreover
often interwoven and all of them are fervently prehended by God in Her lust
for novelty.

VI

Antichrist Psychonaut:
Nietzsche and Psychedelics

> *... And close your eyes with holy dread,*
> *For he on honey-dew hath fed,*
> *And drunk the milk of Paradise.*

So ends the famous fragment of *Kubla Khan* by the Romantic poet, Samuel Taylor Coleridge. He tells us that the poem was an immediate transcription of an opium-induced dream he experienced in 1797. As is known, the Romantic poets and their kin were inspired by the use of psychoactive substances such as opium, the old world's common pain reliever. Pain elimination is its negative advantage, but its positive attribute lies in the psychedelic ('mind-revealing')[1] state it can engender – a state described no better than by the original English opium eater himself, Thomas De Quincey:

> *O just and righteous opium! ... thou bildest upon the bosom*
> *of darkness, out of the fantastic imagery of the brain, cities*
> *and temples, beyond the art of Phidias and Praxiteles –*
> *beyond the splendours of Babylon and Hekatómpylos;*
> *and, "from the anarchy of dreaming sleep," callest into*
> *sunny light the faces of long-buried beauties ... thou hast*
> *the keys of Paradise, O just, subtle, and mighty opium!*[2]

Two decades following the publication of these words the First Opium War commences (1839) in which China is martially punished for trying to hinder the British trade of opium to the Chinese people. Though opium, derived from the innocent garden poppy *Papavar somniferum*, may cradle the keys to Paradise it also clutches the keys to Perdition: its addictive thus potentially ruinous nature is commonly known. Today, partly for these reasons, opiates are mostly illegal without license – stringently so in their most potent forms of morphine and heroin.

Holy dread: the philosopher Friedrich Nietzsche took opium, this milk of Paradise, sometimes confessedly in dangerously high doses. He was also a heavy user of other psychoactive drugs including potassium bromide, a mysterious 'Javanese narcotic', and most unremittingly, chloral hydrate, a known hallucinogen. This narcotic aspect of Nietzsche's life is neglected; it is the aim of this text to reveal the extent of his drug use and its effects, including a report of one of Nietzsche's psychedelic trips. Moreover we shall see how this drug use inspired his philosophy – and how his philosophy inspired this use.

Nietzsche was born in 1844 to a Lutheran pastor who died five years thereafter, at the age of thirty-six, due to a 'softening of the brain'. This fatal malady of his father's was to worry Nietzsche, as a possible hereditary condition, until his own mental collapse in 1889. Friedrich Nietzsche did suffer severe afflictions of the brain and body, beginning in childhood. At the age of thirteen, the severe headaches which were to plague him for the rest of his life began in earnest.[3] So strong were these headaches that near to a whole school semester was lost as the young pupil was prevented from excessive reading by his mother. However, as a bright student, the young Nietzsche surged on and was awarded a place at Schulpforta, a boarding school renowned for its classical studies. Nietzsche wore spectacles as he was very myopic even at this early stage. A doctor in the school once examined his eyes and called attention to the possibility that Nietzsche may go blind at an advanced age.[4] This foresight virtually bore reality, with Nietzsche complaining that in 1879, 'in the thirty-sixth year of life, I arrived at the lowest point of my vitality – I still lived, but without being able to see three paces in front of me.'[5] As Nietzsche's mother, sister, and others believed[6], it was his poor eyesight combined with his lust for reading that caused his initial migraines. To counter the pain, Nietzsche eventually turned to drugs. This in its turn may have exacerbated the problem due to the toxicity, addiction, and withdrawal symptoms those nineteenth century drugs produced.

Nietzsche experimented with drugs early on in life. At the beginning of the 1860s, in Schulpforta, he snorted prohibited *snuff* with his fellow pupil Paul Deussen,[7] and in his fifth year he joined the 'Wild Clique': a fraternal club that endorsed smoking and drinking and spurned studiousness. Nietzsche, however, came to scorn *alcohol* but not before he was demoted from his years-long supervisory position as head of class due to an incident of excessive drinking.[8]

Whilst a student of philology at Leipzig University in 1868, Nietzsche took time out to join the Prussian military machine, training on horseback. As the best rider of the new recruits, he was given the wildest steed to tame. The steed, however, was not for taming: a jump caused Nietzsche a grievous blow to the chest as it cracked into the pommel of the saddle. Ten days of acute pain were relieved by *morphine*.[9]

In 1869, at the mere age of twenty-four, Nietzsche is appointed chair of classical philology at Basel University[10] a month before he is awarded his doctorate (from Leipzig) – awarded, furthermore, without examination. A year later Nietzsche takes leave of his position to serve as a medic in the Franco-Prussian War. He is taught how to administer *chloroform* – a popular anesthetic at the time. After chloroform's discovery in 1831 it was also used recreationally as it produced euphoria. Euphoria, however, was the furthest state of Nietzsche's mind as he treated the war wounded, a depressing mental state that could only have worsened as he himself became ill there. As Nietzsche writes to his friend Karl von Gersdorff:

> *I fell very ill myself and quickly developed a severe attack of dysentery and diphtheria. ... After I had been dosed with* opium *and injections of* tannin *and* silver nitrate *for several days, the worst danger was over.*[11]

As well as contracting these intestinal, bacterial diseases, it is believed that he may have caught syphilis here too, if not in a brothel a few years before. It is a matter of (much) dispute as to whether Nietzsche's general malaise and cognitive downfall in 1889 was caused by this mostly sexually transmitted bacterial infection. As we have seen, however, his headaches had started from a young age, and his father may have passed the problem down to his son. Whatever the case may be, Nietzsche's suffering only increased after 1870 leading to increased drug use to ease the pain. But it was more than pain relief that the drugs caused.

Before Nietzsche had become a professor at Basel, he had become an ardent disciple of the atheist, Idealist philosopher Arthur Schopenhauer. In a sentence, Schopenhauer asserted that the world we perceive is but a human *representation* of the inner essence of everything, which is *will*. Schopenhauer inspired Nietzsche's first published book, *The Birth of Tragedy from the Spirit of Music*, and he arguably returned as inspiration for Nietzsche's later works. As a highly creative individual, Nietzsche could not have overlooked these words from Schopenhauer:

> *By wine or opium we can intensify and considerably*
> *heighten our mental powers, but as soon as the right*
> *measure of stimulus is exceeded, the effect will be exactly*
> *the opposite.*[12]

The double role of opium as a medicinal sedative and as an intellectual, artistic catalyst was well known, and Nietzsche was certainly well aware of the creative possibilities of such substances. In his 1870 essay *The Dionysian Worldview*, a precursor to the extended *Birth of Tragedy*, Nietzsche begins by stating that,

> *There are two states in which man arrives at the*
> *rapturous feeling of existence, namely in dreaming and in*
> *intoxication.*[13]

He then identifies these two states with the gods Apollo and Dionysus, respectively. Loosely speaking, these are in turn identified with Schopenhauer's world of representation and of will. Apollo, commonly adorned with the opium poppy, is valued as signifying ordered beauty, whereas Dionysus, the forest god of wine and trance, is valued as signifying the chaotic drive of unfettered lust and the primal loss of self. In antiquity, Dionysus was regarded as an exotic god who led a procession of bearded satyrs and wild women: the *maenads*. There were a number of Dionysian cults in ancient Greece involving much sex, drugs and loss of control – later to become the orgiastic *Bacchanalia* against which the Roman authorities legislated under threat of death. Under his supposed epithet of *Iacchus*, Dionysus is also closely associated with the *Eleusinian Mysteries*, beloved of those in psychedelic circles. The son of Zeus, Dionysus is reborn after death – a story that bears equivalences to Christ. In Nietzsche's later works, however, Dionysus becomes explicitly equated to the Antichrist, as we shall show. In Nietzsche's early description of the Dionysian state, one cannot help but compare it to a psychoactive drug report with its consequential come down:

> *For the rapture of the Dionysian state with its annihilation*
> *of the ordinary bounds and limits of existence contains,*
> *while it lasts, a lethargic element in which all personal*
> *experience of the past became immersed. This chasm of*
> *oblivion separates the worlds of everyday reality and the*
> *Dionysian reality. But as soon as this everyday reality*

*re-enters consciousness, it is experienced as such, with
nausea: an ascetic, will-negating mood is the fruit of
these states. ... In the consciousness of awakening from
intoxication he sees everywhere the terrible and absurd in
human existence: it nauseates him. Now he understands
the wisdom of the forest god.*[14]

The link between his coinciding opium-treated illnesses in the Franco-
Prussian war and his work on Greek tragedy cannot be overlooked. Indeed
Nietzsche made the connection in the later critical preface/postscript he
produced for his first book, stating that,

> *slowly convalescing from an illness contracted in the field,
> [I] gave definite form to* The Birth of Tragedy...[15]

This book puts forward the theory that the origins of Greek tragedy lie
in the Dionysian chorus that emerged from the older Dionysian mystical
festivals. When fused with the more ordered Apollonian Greek element, the
play structure resulted, with Dionysus at first always the tragic protagonist.
The true Dionysian state that the tragic play sought to symbolize was one
of rapture, of *Rausch*: the rush of intoxication. Thus Nietzsche begins his
philosophical career arguing for the emergence of an art form, Tragedy, from
intoxicated inspiration. Nietzsche's understanding of this state is gleaned from
literature including that of Schopenhauer, and perhaps his own intoxication
at the time. Schopenhauer argued that all individuality is but a representation
(the *principium individuationis*) and that in its essential depths, our individual
will is not separate from the single universal will at the basis of reality. The
Dionysian state causes a dread-inducing fragmentation of one's represented
individuality, conducing a dispersion of oneself into that deeper metaphysical
unity. Nietzsche continues,

> *If we add to this dread the blissful ecstasy which,
> prompted by the same fragmentation of the* principium
> individuationis, *rises up from man's innermost core,
> indeed from nature, we are vouchsafed a glimpse into the
> nature of the Dionysiac, most immediately understandable
> to using the analogy of intoxication. Under the influence
> of the narcotic potion hymned by all primitive men and
> peoples, or in the powerful approach of spring, joyfully*

> *penetrating the whole of nature, those Dionysiac urges*
> *are awakened, and as they grow more intense, subjectivity*
> *becomes a complete forgetting of the self.*[16]

In his later postscripted preface to the book, Nietzsche argues that this Dionysian 'madness' might be a 'neurosis of health' – that is, a *healthy madness* which would only appear to be an oxymoron to a culture in decline. In this added section he writes,

> *Might visions and hallucinations not have been shared by*
> *whole communities, by whole cult gatherings? And what*
> *if ... it was madness itself, to use a phrase of Plato's, that*
> *brought the greatest blessings upon Greece?*[17]

Hence Nietzsche, from the outset, was enthused about narcotic, psychedelic intoxication and its value, whilst simultaneously he himself was becoming increasingly intoxicated as his illness progressed.

Progress it did: severe insomnia, stomach and intestinal pains, eyestrain and increasing blindness creeps up upon his person. In 1876 he is granted a long period of absence from Basel due to his sickness. Many of his personal letters complain of his ailments, to the extent that one judges him to be a 'justified hypochondriac', if that also be not an oxymoron. In 1879 he was forced to completely end his professorship and life at Basel University due to frequent and excessive headaches, nausea, vomiting and seizures.[18] As a result, Nietzsche was now free to pursue an unlimited life of philosophy, which had progressively become his ideal.

Though he left, his ailments did not. The beginning of the 1880s were in fact his most intense period of pain. As well as suffering physiologically, he was saddened by the loss of his friendship with Lou Salomé and Paul Rée. Just before he begins to write what he considered to be his masterpiece, *Thus Spoke Zarathustra*,[19] he writes to his two formerly close friends the following:

> *My dears, Lou and Rée:*
> *... Consider me, the two of you, as a semilunatic with a sore*
> *head who has been totally bewildered by long solitude. To*
> *this, I think, sensible insight into the state of things I have*
> *come after taking a huge dose of opium – in desperation.*
> *But instead of losing my reason as a result, I seem at last*
> *to have come to reason. ...*[20]

Over a decade later Lou Salomé writes in her book, *Friedrich Nietzsche in seinen Werken*, that intoxication and dreams were a central inspiration to Nietzsche's life and philosophy. She writes,

> *Nietzsche ... was convinced that especially during conditions of intoxication and dream, a fullness of the past could be revived in the individual's present. Dreams always played a great role in his life and thinking, and during his last years he often drew from them – as with the solution of a riddle – the contents of his teachings. In this manner he employed, for instance, the dream related in Zarathustra (II, "The Soothsayer"), which came to him in the fall of 1882 in Leipzig; he never tired of carrying it about him and interpreting it.*[21]

With his concurrent opium use one can compare the inspiration derived from such opium-induced dreaming with that of the Romantics, to whom Nietzsche was ostensibly averse. Nietzsche was also, famously, averse to *alcohol* – which he compared unfavourably to opiates in his 1882 book, *The Joyous Science*:

> *Perhaps Asians are distinguished above Europeans by a capacity for longer, deeper calm; even their opiates have a slow effect and require patience, as opposed to the disgusting suddenness of the European poison, alcohol.*[22]

The reverence and inspiration that Nietzsche derives from opium can also be witnessed in the second edition of that same work, in two poems inspired by poppy-derived opium:

> *... Only on my bed flailed,*
> *Poppy and good conscience, those*
> *Trusted soporifics, failed. ...*
>
> *One hour passed, or two, or three–*
> *Or a year? – when suddenly*
> *All my thoughts and mind were drowned*
> *In timeless monotony:*
> *An abyss without a ground*
> *Opened up – not one more sound. ...*[23]

Such opium pipe-dream poetry ranks alongside those of the Kubla Khan clan. In a subsequent poem, Nietzsche poses the problem of his pain with provision of poppies:

> *... Pain writes with daggers that are flying*
> *Into my bones:*
> *"World has no heart;*
> *The fool bears her a grudge and groans."*
>
> *Pour poppies, pour,*
> *O fever! Poison in my brain!*
> *You test my brow too long with pain.*
> *Why do you ask, "For what reward?" ...*
>
> *You fever, I should bless?–* [24]

Nietzsche's ills were treated by him as both a superficial curse and as a deeper blessing. It was the ailments that necessitated the opiates and other drugs, which in turn further inspired his thought. A physiologically healthy Nietzsche may have dissipated into the shadows of history. In this respect his drug use was a vital condition of his profound, earth-shattering philosophy which uncovered and uprooted the morbidly entrenched covert legacy of Christianity in western society.

Nietzsche pushed himself to, and perhaps beyond, the limits of human intellectualization. To fuel this heroic drive even opium-injected dreams may not have sufficed. As Lou Salomé, to whom Nietzsche twice proposed, continued to write in her biography of the man:

> *And yet, the tranquil dream is insufficient for that quest.*
> *What is needed is a much more real, effective, and even*
> *more terrible experiencing, namely through orgiastic*
> *Dionysian conditions and the chaos of frenzied passions*
> *– yes madness itself as a means of sinking back down*
> *into the mass of entwined feelings and imaginings. This*
> *seemed for Nietzsche the last road into the primal depths*
> *imbedded within us.*
>
> *Quite early Nietzsche had brooded over the meaning of*
> *madness as a possible source for knowledge and its inner*
> *sense that may have led the ancients to discern a sign of*
> *divine election.*[25]

Did Nietzsche seek to induce divine madness so as to fully intuit the depths of the psyche? With this in mind, his famous maxim "What does not kill you makes you stronger"[26] takes on a form applicable to the intake of psychoactive substances. Did Nietzsche take hazardous mixes and doses of psychoactive drugs? Yes. It may have made his philosophy stronger, but it may have killed him as a philosopher too – this was certainly the view of his mother:

> *He used all the sleeping medications that have ever been invented, said the professors. His worst one was chloral. That one practically killed him.*[27]

Chloral, and its admixture with water, *chloral hydrate*, was a common sedative in the nineteenth century, now a controlled substance. More than opium, this drug appears to be Nietzsche's preferred poison. In a letter to his friend and former colleague, Franz Overbeck, he writes in 1883:

> *I realized that in the last two months I have consumed 50 grams of chloral hydrate (pure). I never slept without this drug! But I have slept, now, after fourteen days in a row - oh what bliss!*[28]

In one of her biographies of her brother, Elisabeth Förster-Nietzsche – who at times took care of Nietzsche – remonstrates against his abuse of chloral:

> *In the winter of 1882–3, owing to that terrible influenza, he had for the first time used chloral regularly, in large doses. He was so unfavourably impressed with its peculiar effects that in the spring of 1883 he did his best to cure himself of the habit. ... [When] he took chloral before going to bed, it led next morning to a curiously excitable condition, in which men and things appeared to him in a totally false light. Towards noon, he thought, this condition vanished, and more "philanthropic sentiments" returned. Accordingly he had become very careful, although the sleep produced by chloral seems to have been remarkably pleasant – not dull and heavy but filled with delightful dreams. ... If only he had kept to this one drug, however, the result might have been less serious.*[29]

So his mother and sister both maintained that it was the effect of large doses and mixtures of drugs that brought Nietzsche his cognitive ruin, his madness.[30] Chloral hydrate was synthesised in 1832, and since 1869 had been used for hypnotic or sedative purposes, i.e. for sleep induction and pain relief. It is now known to be potentially hazardous with a risk of death in the case of intoxication. It is not commonly considered a psychedelic drug, yet it can produce visions and auditory 'hallucinations'.

One of Nietzsche's students reported that,

> *Insomnia, which was not improved by repeated overwork, by* chloral *or* potassium bromide, *but made worse excruciating headaches, and other neuralgic ailments, tormented his life.*[31]

Potassium bromide is an anticonvulsant (anti-seizure) and sedative drug, and is used today in veterinary practice, and in Germany is still administered to human beings. Nietzsche's dual use of chloral and potassium bromide is notable because it was this combination that led to the bewildering experiences of the English author Evelyn Waugh. These effects affected him to such a degree that they provide the content to his peculiar autobiographical work, *The Ordeal of Gilbert Pinfold*. This concocted sleeping-draught caused auditory and conceptual hallucinations, often in a terrifying manner, with voices suggesting suicide. When Waugh was admitted to St Bartholomew's Hospital for treatment, his regular chloral was immediately withdrawn and replaced with paraldehyde, a move that immediately stopped the hallucinations.[32]

The well-known neurologist Oliver Sacks has also written of the psychedelic experiences that chloral hydrate caused him:

> *Depressed and insomniac, I was taking ever-increasing amounts of chloral hydrate to get to sleep, and was up to fifteen times the usual dose every night. ... [But] for the first time in several months I went to bed without my usual knockout dose. ... [Upon] waking, I found myself excruciatingly sensitive to sounds. ... I went across the road, as I often did, for a cup of coffee and a sandwich. As I was stirring the coffee it suddenly turned green, then purple. I looked up, startled, and saw a huge proboscidean head, like an elephant seal. Panic seized me; I slammed*

a five-dollar note on the table and ran across the road to
a bus on the other side. But all the passengers on the bus
seemed to have smooth white heads like giant eggs, with
huge glittering eyes like the faceted compound eyes of
insects – their eyes seemed to move in sudden jerks, which
increased the feeling of their fearfulness and alienness.[33]

In the end Sacks discovered that it was the fact that he had stopped taking chloral that caused the hallucinations, a case of *delirium tremens*. Thus we see that chloral hydrate is addictive, toxic, and directly and posteriorly hallucinatory. Taken in large doses and mixed with other drugs, the effects can only be potent. There is an account of a psychedelic experience Nietzsche had in mid-August 1884. His friend Resa von Schirnhofer decided to visit Nietzsche in Sils-Maria, Switzerland. After an absence of one and a half days, von Schirnhofer ventures to his house and is led into the dining room – then:

As I stood waiting by the table, the door to the adjacent
room on the right opened, and Nietzsche appeared. With a
distraught expression on his pale face, he leaned wearily
against the post of the half-opened door and immediately
began to speak about the unbearableness of his ailment. He
described to me how, when he closed his eyes, he saw an
abundance of fantastic flowers, winding and intertwining,
constantly growing and changing forms and colours in
exotic luxuriance, sprouting one out of the other. "I never
get any rest," he complained...[34]

Von Schirnhofer also tells of Nietzsche's unorthodox and deviant means of acquiring his drugs:

In Rapallo and in other places of the Riviera di Levante,
where he had spent his times of worst health, he had written
for himself all kinds of prescriptions signed Dr Nietzsche,
which had been prepared and filled without question or
hesitation. Unfortunately I took no notes and the only one
I remember is chloral hydrate. But since Nietzsche, as he
expressly told me, had been surprised never to be asked
whether he was a medical doctor authorized to prescribe
this kind of medication, I conclude that some dubious
medicines must have been among them.[35]

So Nietzsche, a user of the addictive substance opium since at least 1870, a heavy chloral hydrate user, and a proponent of the intoxicated Dionysian state, uses his doctoral title to prescribe himself the drugs he wants. If ever the term *drug fiend* were applied to a true philosopher, Nietzsche would fit the case. 'Psychonaut' certainly fits, a name coined by philosopher Ernst Jünger,[36] whom Heidegger called 'the only genuine continuer of Nietzsche'.[37] Von Schirnhofer speculated over whether Nietzsche also used hashish, stating that his intensive reading of French authors must have included Charles Baudelaire who wrote of hashish and opium trances in *Artificial Paradises*, and in *The Flowers of Evil*.

In *Ecce Homo*, his autobiography, Nietzsche writes,

> *If one wants to get free from an unendurable pressure one*
> *needs hashish. Very well, I needed Wagner.*[38]

This suggests Nietzsche was not a hashish user, at least not a frequent one. But with Nietzsche's somewhat haughty position, his belief in a necessary 'pathos of distance'[39] between people, and his championing of great men of intellect and art, he must have felt endeared and perhaps tempted by Baudelaire's words on the drug:

> *I am not asserting that hashish produces in all men all of*
> *the [fantastical] effects I have described here. I have more*
> *or less recounted the phenomena generally produced,*
> *except for a few variations, among individuals of artistic*
> *and philosophical bent. ... But there are others in whom the*
> *drug raises only a raucous madness, a violent merriment*
> *resembling vertigo ... [yet it can conduce] the extreme*
> *development of the poetic mind...*[40]

Whether or not Nietzsche took hashish he certainly exhibited an extreme development of the poetic mind. In a passage in his autobiography, Nietzsche speaks of the singular, overwhelming type of inspiration with which he is bequeathed. Though he does not connect Nietzsche's 'inspiration' to his drug use, the Nietzsche biographer Curtis Cate asserts of this passage that 'his description of the hallucinating moments of inspiration during which he felt powerless and "possessed" merits a place in any good anthology of mystical experiences'.[41] When we consider the view that psychedelic experiences *are* mystical experiences, in the vein of William James' varieties thereof,[42] we can agree with this assessment. As we saw with Waugh and Sacks, chloral hydrate can cause auditory and visual hallucinations, a drug we know Nietzsche self-prescribed and used in high doses. It is highly plausible then that Nietzsche's 'inspiration' was drug-induced hallucination – and no less valuable for that. In fact, his revelations can be witnessed as testimony to the potential supreme value of psychedelic chemicals within the right mind:

> *Has anyone at the end of the nineteenth century a distinct conception of what poets of strong ages called* inspiration*? ... If one had the slightest residue of superstition left in one, one would hardly be able to set aside the idea that one is merely incarnation, merely mouthpiece, merely medium of overwhelming forces. The concept of revelation, in the sense that something suddenly, with unspeakable certainty and subtlety, becomes* visible, *audible, something that shakes and overturns one to the depths, simply describes the fact. One hears, one does not seek; one takes, one does not ask who gives; a thought flashes up like lightning, with necessity, unfalteringly formed – I have never had any choice. An ecstasy whose tremendous tension sometimes discharges itself in a flood of tears, whilst one's steps now involuntarily rush along, now involuntarily lag; a complete being outside of oneself with the distinct consciousness of a multitude of subtle shudders and trickles down to one's toes; a depth of happiness in which the most painful and gloomy things appear ... Everything is in the highest degree involuntary but takes place as in a tempest of a feeling of freedom, of absoluteness, of power, of divinity. ... This is* my *experience of inspiration; I do not doubt that one has to go back thousands of years to find anyone who could say to me "it is mine also".*[43]

As Lou Salomé intimated, Nietzsche may have pushed himself to the edge of madness to overcome the common condition of man to taste divinity. Was it his psychedelic inspiration that caused both his psychological apotheosis and his physiological downfall? With regard to his downfall, his sister believed that,

> *The correct diagnosis, perhaps, would be this: a brain*
> *exhausted by overstrain of the nerves of head and eye that*
> *could no longer resist taking drugs to excess, and thus*
> *became disabled.*[44]

Nietzsche's infamous[45] sister also describes another drug that she blamed for his stroke into mental destruction in 1889: the *Javanese narcotic*:

> *Above all I regard two sleeping draughts, chloral and*
> *Javanese narcotic, as responsible for his paralytic stroke*
> *... [In] 1884, so far as I remember, he got to know a*
> *Dutchman, who recommended him a Javanese narcotic,*
> *and presented him with a fairly large bottle ... The stuff*
> *tasted like rather strong alcohol and had an outlandish*
> *smell ... The Dutchman impressed us with the fact that only*
> *a few drops should be taken at a time in a glass of water.*
> *I tried it, and observed a somewhat exhilarating effect. ...*
> *Later, in the autumn of 1885, he confessed to me that on*
> *one occasion he had taken a few drops too much, with the*
> *result that he suddenly threw himself to the ground in a*
> *fit of convulsive laughter. ... During the early days of his*
> *insanity he used often to say in confidence to our mother*
> *that he "had taken twenty drops" (he did not mention of*
> *what), and that his brain had then "gone off the track." ...*
> *Perhaps the worst of it all was that he used both chloral*
> *and the Javanese drug at the same time.*[46]

The island of Java was part of the colonized Dutch East Indies. In 1875 coca plants were introduced to Java, eventually leading to the *Nederlandsche Cocaïne Fabriek* in 1900, the year of Nietzsche's death. The Javanese coca leaf was not as potent as its Peruvian sibling in Nietzsche's time, but it was cheaper.[47] The Javanese narcotic his sister spoke of thus likely contained traces of *cocaine*, and possibly the assorted herbs of the traditional Indonesian healing concoction *Jamu*. It would be unconvincing that combining this combination with chloral, opium, potassium bromide, etc., would *not* lead to hallucinations, madness, mental breakdown, and apotheosis: Nietzsche signed off final letters of 1889 with the name Dionysus,[48] whom he had recently identified as the Antichrist:

*Who knows the true name of the Antichrist? – with the
name of a Greek god: I called it the Dionysiac.*[49]

In Nietzsche's mature work, Dionysus becomes the representation of
the overman figure: a type that affirms and revels in pain and destruction,
the polar contrary to the Christian type who only values joy in peace and
comfort. In 1888 Nietzsche exclaims:

*Affirmation of life even in its strangest and sternest
problems, the will to life rejoicing in its own inexhaustibility
through the sacrifice of its highest types – that is what I
called Dionysian ... beyond pity and terror, to realize in
oneself the eternal joy of becoming – that joy which also
encompasses joy in destruction ... I am the last disciple of
the philosopher Dionysus.*[50]

After *The Birth of Tragedy*, Dionysus returns to Nietzsche's philosophy
in 1886 in *Beyond Good and Evil*. Now, rather than subservient to
Schopenhauer's unwitting Christian values, Dionysus represents Nietzsche's
radical revaluation of those values that lie hidden beneath western culture,
and thus does Dionysus denote a new form of thinking – without doubt a
dangerous form to many. In this extreme opposition to such sacerdotal
ideology, one understands why Dionysus *is* the Antichrist, both of whom *are*
Nietzsche. He is the Antichrist Psychonaut: his pagan philosopher forest god
of intoxication *speaks* to him – perhaps in the mode of his aforementioned
'inspiration', or black revelation:

*"...I often think how I can help [mankind] go forward and
make them stronger, deeper, and more evil than they are."
"Stronger, deeper, and more evil?" I asked, frightened.
"Yes," he said once again, "stronger, deeper, and more
evil – more beautiful too." And at that the tempter god
smiled his halcyon smile, as if he had just uttered a
charming compliment.*[51]

A new Dionysian cult based on Nietzsche's reformulation of the god
might very well suffer the same capital jurisdictive fate as that which befell
its Roman predecessors. Whatever the future yields, Nietzsche's philosophy
will be a significant factor thereof. His philosophy has already, a century on,

had a decisive impact upon history. That this philosophy was provoked, in a degree hitherto undiagnosed, by reveries occasioned by chemical measures exposes one to the realization of the great power of these substances, powers guiding history. Nietzsche risked himself, his sanity, his life, so to touch the heavens and taste the Hades of human mentality – he may thereby have destroyed himself. But destruction is a joy to Dionysus, a deity who shall be born again.

VII

Neo-Nihilism:
the Philosophy of Power

Introduction

All cultures operate with ideology, so ubiquitous as to be invisible to those within, but blatant to those without. This is apparent when one looks upon the seemingly absurd virtues and vices of past ages and far places. What is also, however, seemingly apparent is that one's present ideology, ultimately one's morality, is somehow correct, others' being incorrect. In the West, we think we have 'progressed' morally from former, less moral times. But this is false; we have simply changed: moral progress and retrogress are illusions. In this sense, morality is more akin to fashion than to technology.

It is most often the case that setting faith in the ethics of one's culture serves one's interests. Therefore this text will not be of service to that majority; the information herein is too potent for that character. If such a conformer sets his sight upon the light here offered he will only be capable of reaction rather than assimilation, as is purpose – the same sun can be both enlightening and carcinogenic. The author asks you to set aside as much you can current ideologies held, only in order to advance yourself, to understand your surrounding influences. Nihilism, in the sense in which it is used here, means that there exist no objective morals, no absolute good nor evil. This idea goes far and transcends modern cultural relativism, to depths and darknesses only visited hitherto by a brave few adventurers. Without the characteristic of courage you will not understand, you will not want to understand.

As prolegomena to the three chapters following, let us begin with the first: Morality as Illusion. We know in the modern world that religion is illusion, power structures presented as divine truths with omnipotent and transcendent sanctions. Morality is likewise such an illusion, presented as fact but in fact another such power structure. As the sanction of morality can no longer be God, we assume there must be a secular replacement – in vain. There is no sanction. There is no God. There is no prescriptive morality. Morality exists like religion exists, neither contains truths. Moreover morality is not even useful in many cases, it is a hindrance. The sooner one absorbs this truth the sooner one's liberty awakens.

Secondly, we are born into an old hierarchy of laws, and taught that obedience thereto is not only to our benefit but that transgression will be met with physical force, which is also in our interest. We do not debate law, we debate laws; as if our subservience to external authority was without question, a default position. In Europe physical force is the prerogative of the state, not of the individual. As there is no morality, there is no basis for law, and thus all law is one unit of people ruling over others by force. We humans are still animals; our intellect merely provides greater expedients to that same brute nature. It is in the interest of rulers to disguise their rule as common sense, a Leviathan that cannot be challenged – much as the rule of the Church in medieval times.

Thirdly, if law be based on morality, and morality on power, then power is the bedrock of human affairs. Life is the will to power. This later concept, *Wille zur Macht*, blooms in the works of Friedrich Nietzsche, but buds in Schopenhauer. In the latter, all life, and all matter, is the representation of will or force in varying degrees of complexity. Only in ourselves is this will not only a representation but known in-itself as our desire. For Schopenhauer this constant striving of desire causes only suffering: need, disappointment and boredom. For Nietzsche this drive may cause pain but he does not consider pain to be inimical to life. Conversely he considers pain to be a catalyst to life: 'what does not kill you makes you stronger', as he famously exclaimed. This drive, this will, this force, is a drive to grow, develop, expand, advance – in sum to gain power: 'the will to power'. In most individuals this is performed at the subconscious level. To claim that power seeking is immoral is to seek power. When we accept that life is will to power, our consciousness will align itself with our subconscious, thereby providing a tonic harmony. Nihilism is the key to liberty and power.

Morality is Illusion

There are innumerable collections of texts devoted to the issue of morality, the majority of which are unfounded sentimentalist ramblings. Most of it enquires as to the foundation of morality; not much enquires as to whether such a foundation exists. We do not ask what the evidence for God's existence is, we ask whether God's existence has such evidence at all. We do not ask what the meaning of life is but whether such a meaning exists. We must extend this foundational questioning to ethics.

The great mass of error with regard to moral theory is caused by the conflation of *descriptive* and *prescriptive* morality. No one doubts that moralities, like religions, exist. We can describe those moralities in terms of behaviour, belief, biological and cultural origination, etc. For example, in Viking-age Scandinavia it was believed that a cold, compassion-free heart was a virtue and that heaven, Valhalla, was only available to those who died in battle. In ancient Sparta, Lacedaemon, theft was only immoral if one was caught. Slavery was accepted, as was wife-exchange. Infanticide of the disabled was considered a moral imperative; weakness, a vice. We can seek to explain these ethical standards by appealing to the tribalistic culture in which they operated and the biological inheritance of aggression, intelligence, etc. Such a historical, global, scientific and cultural overview of the moralities that have existed and do exist is *descriptive* morality and morality as such is logically legitimate.

However, the logic falters when moral imperatives – oughts, shoulds, duties – are derived from moral descriptions or facts. Because one acts in a certain way due to certain dispositions does not logically imply that one, or others, *ought* to act in that way. A person may have a disposition to aggression (a characteristic), but this does not imply that he ought to be aggressive. Likewise, a person may have a disposition to humility and compassion, but this too does not imply that he or others ought to be humble and compassionate. As the great Scot David Hume made clear, one cannot derive an *ought* from an *is*, a *value* from a *fact*, a *prescription* from a *description*. This is known as the *is-ought gap*, or *Hume's Guillotine*. Many such decapitations have resulted since his death in 1776, though hidden from the eyes of the many.

As a means logically implies an end, so an *ought* can only logically come from an if-clause: for instance, "I ought to exercise *if* I want to build my strength." Often the if-clause is omitted in ink or sound, but it is always implied: "She ought to diet (if she wants to lose weight)." The if-clause is essentially the purpose of an act (strengthening, thinning). But, as the existentialists realised, without God there is no objective purpose for a human. The purpose of a knife is to cut, therefore it ought to be sharp. A knife has a purpose as it was designed by man with the purpose in mind. But man himself was not designed, his complexity is explained not by creation but by evolution, as was argued by Empedocles in the Iron Age. Thus, without a god, man has no purpose, there is no absolute meaning to life. But with no purpose, there is no objective, universal if-clause and consequently no objective, universal ought-clause – no absolute morality. All *oughts* are conditioned by an *if, because all means necessarily imply an end.* The bones of morality lie within God's tomb.

Despite this indubitable logic, atheist Christians, as it were, try to argue that mankind does have an objective purpose from which values, *oughts*, can be issued. Often one hears that we have evolved to be social and friendly animals, and thus we ought to be amicable. There are two main errors in this. Firstly is the fact that we have also evolved aggression and tribalism from which contrary *oughts* can be derived by the same principle. Secondly, even if virtually every person had the same amicable nature, one still could not derive a value from this supposed fact, an *ought* from an *is*, a *prescription* from a *description* – due to Hume's Guillotine. A person, a lone wolf, who acted contrary to the generally desired will for amicability could not be said to be wrong, only unusual. One could not logically say to that person that he ought to do this or that, because that ought would be conditioned by an if-clause, a purpose that the wolf did not share. Again, there is no absolute, universal, objective if-clause – no absolute purpose to life. There are only subjective, personal purposes.

As a side-note against those who would claim that there exist certain shared values amongst all peoples, one firstly points out that this is not descriptively true. Secondly, and more importantly, even were it true, one could not derive a prescriptive morality from this because if everyone shared the same values, then prescriptive morality would be pointless: one would not need to tell people how to behave if they already did so. Prescriptive morality is only necessary when other people act contrary to the way that one would desire them to behave.

Ultimately all oughts are based on desire or sentiment, not on reason. The if-clause is based on desire, which is not objective, true for all. Therefore all prescriptive, or normative, morality is the sought imposition of one person or group's desire over another. Morality is a power structure. Even if the desire is harmony and peace, this is not a purpose shared by all. The Heroic societies of ages past offer themselves as examples of those whose purpose differs from the modern world. Glory in battle, valour, honour were frequently preferred as purpose than the perceived decadence and decrepitude of peace and harmony. Today these cultures are often viewed through a glass darkly as 'immoral'. But that is only because the purpose of life is considered to be something different from theirs, and moreover more 'correct' than theirs. But the mistake here lies in the belief that a desire can be correct or incorrect – a desire is a state of mind and body; only a proposition, or an action or form according to a purpose, can be correct or not. It is not contrary to reason to prefer, to have a subjective desire for, violence rather than peace, chaos to order. It is a psychological rather than logical matter. The if-clause, the purpose, cannot be incorrect, wrong, no matter how unusual or unpopular. For precisely this reason does Hume state that "Tis not contrary to reason to prefer the destruction of the whole world to the scratching of my finger.'

An *ought* can only come from an *if*; an *ought* can never come from an *is*. The if-clause is the purpose of an action; the ought-clause reveals the means to attain that purpose; the attainment of the purpose is called 'good'; the failure of attainment is called 'bad'. The etymology of these words reveals differing uses, but the logic remains the same. A good knife is one that attains its purpose of cutting well; a bad knife fails to achieve this purpose – through bluntness, etc. So a 'good' action is one that attains its purpose well. A 'good person' is one who attains his purpose well. But as mankind has no purpose, there is no such thing as 'a good person'. This term only refers to a person whose beliefs and actions conform to another person's desired purpose for mankind. Thus, as people's desires differ here, the same individual will be considered good by one person and bad by another. Neither of the two opinions are correct or incorrect, it is only a matter of perspective without any objective standard. 'There is nothing either good or bad – but thinking makes it so,' as the Bard of Avon recognised.

It must be understood that this understanding is not, and cannot lead to, 'cultural relativism': the view that all cultures are equally valid and so criticism of them ought not occur. This view is quite prevalent today in the West by those wishing themselves to be peering from the moral pedestal. The fallacy here is contradiction: 'there are no objective oughts, therefore one ought not criticize another culture or creed.' The second *ought* contradicts the first. As there are no objective *oughts*, to claim one ought not criticise another culture cannot be objectively true. This imperative is actually based on the desire to curtail other people's expressed desires – desire against desire, nothing more. Although another culture's values may not be objectively incorrect, they can transgress one's own desires and so can be disparaged as undesirable rather than incorrect, to serve oneself.

This understanding, nihilism, also undermines another very popular moral theory: Utilitarianism: the view that what is good is that which yields the greatest happiness for the greatest number. Utilitarianism has two presuppositions that it cannot justify, *viz*. that all people ought to be treated as equals (when weighing pleasure or pain) and that happiness is good. The first presupposition has a redundant theistic if-clause: if we want to follow

God's commands via Jesus' Golden Rule. God's fall brings down the absolute sanction of this egalitarian rule. The Golden Rule, 'all things whatsoever ye would that men should do to you, do ye even so to them', not originating from Christianity but mostly proliferated therefrom, is very helpful to those who are in an inferior position as its command would increase their standing, their power. But from someone in a superior position, this rule would decrease their relative standing. For such a reason does Nietzsche call Christianity a slave morality. Indeed Nietzsche saw Christianity as a power structure emanating from the weak as a system that conforms to their type's subjective desire. The extent of this desire overwhelmed the Romans, causing their downfall. So victorious was this hostile takeover that such a subjective sentiment was ingrained as objective fact and 'common sense'. This religious takeover set its roots so deeply into man's consciousness that today morality is considered only to be Christian morality, even if one is not consciously a Christian. Thus the need for this very text to worm out those rotten talons.

There have existed on earth many moralities, history emancipates us from 'common sense' and prejudice, if that be desired. The second presupposition, that happiness is good, is also not an objective fact unless considered a tautology, and if so it is merely the analysis of a given definition, a definition that can be changed without contradiction of course. 'Happiness is bad' is not necessarily a contradiction. As written previously, happiness as end has not always been considered good but quite the opposite, as a sign of decadence and decay. Logically, 'good' means the attainment of a purpose. So 'happiness is good' if it attains a purpose. But the purpose is subjective, personal. Therefore to state that happiness is good can never be an objective fact. Furthermore, happiness can involve the unhappiness of others, as expressed by the German word *Schadenfreude*, in which case claiming happiness to be good, something to be attained, would contradict the first presupposition that one ought to treat others as equals. Utilitarianism cannot justify its foundational principle, despite Mill's attempt to do so via the use of the conscience. An absurd attempt as the conscience's pronouncements are considered good which merely postpones the error: Why is it good? What purpose does it seek to attain? Is that purpose objective? No, farewell.

Utilitarianism is in essence a form of Christian morality that suffers identity crisis. Kant's moral theory, Deontology, also suffers this ailment. It will suffice to say against Kant, generally genius in his thought, that he presupposes an Aristotelian teleology: that everything has a purpose, and that the purpose of reason, a good will, presupposes what 'good' is as a foundation for arguing what goodness is – thereby begging the question. A 'good will' for

Kant is indistinguishable from a Christian subjective preference. Furthermore, the great Prussian simply assumes that morality must be prescriptive and thereafter seeks to find postulates that would maintain this view – namely free will, immortality of the soul and God. One merely denies the first assumption as being without reason or evidence to deny the three consequent conditions. Though a post- Kantian generally, Schopenhauer rejected Kant's moral theory in likewise fashion: 'Kant's first false statement lies in his concept of ethics itself, a concept which we find articulated most clearly [in the Metaphysics of Morals]: "In a practical philosophy it is not a concern to indicate reasons for what happens, but laws for what ought to happen, even if it never happens." – This is already a decided *petitio principii* [question begging]. Who told you that there are laws to which we ought to subject our actions? Who told you that something ought to happen that never happens? – What justifies your assuming this beforehand and thereupon immediately to press upon us an ethics in a legislative-imperative form as the only possible sort?' (*On the Basis of Morals*, §4.)

Contractarianism is another false idol worshipped by the masses that is easily refuted. This moral theory claims that values derive from actions that instill peace and stability in society such as altruism, charity, law-abidance, etc., as it is in everyone's interest. We all sign an unwritten contract to behave thus that pays off. However, it assumes values in order to prove values, thereby begging the question, assuming what it seeks to prove. It assumes that peace and stability are objective values, values that all would desire, in order to conclude that values that induce peace and stability, such as being non-violent and a 'good citizen', are correct. But if one does not consider peace and stability to be values in themselves then the consequent values neither follow. A person may prefer a life of adventure, war, risk, to a life of comfortable conformism. As such what he ought to do, his values, will differ greatly from the average man – and he will not be wrong, 'immoral', but simply different.

Contractarianism also presupposes equality as a value, as will shortly be explained, thereby substantiating egalitarian values. But equality is not an objective value, and is chiefly a tool for those who have lower status, or for those who desire the backing of these ranks to overpower an opposing force. The most pernicious example of this mistake is the American philosopher John Rawls' 'veil of ignorance' concept. He believed that an issue could be determined as moral or not if one imagined that one had to create a society without knowing one's role in that society – wearing the 'veil of ignorance'. Naturally, he claimed, one would forbid all forms of inequality as one could suffer it oneself. But it seems his veil also forbade him from seeing logic. If one wants an equal, egalitarian, society one would wear the veil of ignorance. If one did not want an egalitarian society, one would not wear it. And one could not retort that not wanting to wear it was immoral, as the concept 'immoral' is founded on choosing to wear the veil. Rawls *et al.* presuppose that equality is good in order to prove equality is good: a serpent that bites its own tail.

Another popular ethical system in America, with the misnomer 'Objectivism', coined and fabricated by the novelist Ayn Rand also suffers error. She talks about the 'virtues of selfishness' whereas a little selflessness would suit her the better. She believed that the is-ought gap could be bridged by arguing that the will to survive is a fact, an *is*, from which an *ought* can be derived; and since we all share this will to survive, we all ought to ensure our survival – from which a theory of selfishness emerges: 'The fact that a living entity is, determines what it ought to do. So much for the relation between "is" and "ought"', she writes. The is-clause here becomes the if-clause: if I want to survive, I ought to do x, y and z. But the initial error lies in the assumption that the will to survive is the aim of life. The frequency of suicide betrays the fact that there must be another aim transcending survival. But the more pointed and important error is in not realising that a condition for a set is not by necessity a member of that set. A condition for thunder is lightning, but this does not entail that lightning is thunder; a condition for a tree is light, but this does not entail that light is a tree. Likewise, a condition for values is life, but this does not entail that life is a value. If one erroneously accepted that a condition for a set is necessarily a member of that set, one would have to accept that as life is also a condition for disvalues, life is thus also a disvalue. The contradiction that emerges from this acceptance – that life is both a value and a disvalue – exposes the underlying logic as flawed. Furthermore, Rand misunderstands Hume's is-ought gap thereby effacing her criticism of it. Hume's is-ought gap, 'Hume's Guillotine', is that objective values cannot be derived from objective facts. Rand's example that one *ought* to value life as life *is*, it exists, merely means that a subjective value (often one's own life) comes from an objective fact (that one exists). But Hume and nihilists accept this. Moralists, such as Rand, want to claim objective values from objective facts, which is impossible. Values are not objective – so much for Objectivism.

What emerges from all this is the realisation that many atheists are hesitant to admit: that without God there is no prescriptive morality. Again, from Schopenhauer: 'I recognise no other source [for prescriptive morality] than the Decalogue [the Ten Commandments, Exodus 20]. In general, in the centuries of Christianity, philosophical ethics has unconsciously taken its form from the theological. Since this ethics is now essentially dictatorial, the philosophical too, has appeared in the form of prescription ... without suspecting that for this, first a further authority is necessary [God]. Instead, it supposes that this is its own and natural form' (*ibid.*). Many if not most atheists take this as a criticism of atheism as they have not the strength to give up too many shackles. It is not a criticism, it is a fact to be acknowledged and celebrated. But in a culture that bases its order on the objectivity of ethics, to stray too far from this order is a liability that threatens reprimand. Most individuals cannot handle independence of thought, it presents itself as too difficult and dangerous – 'Few are made for independence – it is a prerogative of the strong', writes Schopenhauer's 'successor', Nietzsche.

Those so-called atheists who try to base prescriptive morality on biology are guilty of the aforementioned conflation of descriptive and prescriptive morality, a conflation that costs them their authority. Those who argue that morality comes from evolution: that we have evolved sympathy and altruism and that we therefore ought to be sympathetic and altruistic fall into the is-ought gap. That we have evolved these characteristics is not in question. But that we ought to follow them is. The characteristics are descriptions. But these descriptions are then magically transformed into prescriptions. One could equally validly (i.e. not validly) prescribe envy as it too is a characteristic which we have evolved. Aggression and violence have also evolved, else we would not exhibit these tendencies. Both 'good' and 'evil' (in the traditional sense) have evolved.

To prescribe those characteristics we describe as 'good' implies that the prescriber already assumes a morality in order to prescribe that same morality. The moral evolutionist assumes, as default, that Christian slave characteristics are good and then tries to explain how those characteristics evolved without God. But he is ignorant of the fact that his initial selection of values was predetermined by an anterior morality which, in the West, was Christianity. He is unwittingly propagating a morality sanctioned by a dead God. This is, in truth, the greatest victory of the religion: people believe and follow its creed without believing in its foundation. It is understandable that two millennia of a religion will entrench itself in a people's mode of thinking, but two millennia is enough.

If morality is then an illusion, why do the great multitude believe it? The same question could be asked of religion, and similar answers could be returned. Divine faith has benefits for both the creators and followers.

It is propagated by the priestly caste for their maintenance and power; it is followed by a flock as it offers consolation and seeming explanation of the unknown. This symbiotic relationship is mirrored in normative, prescriptive, morality. The secular priests of today, predominantly a bourgeoisie, maintain authority and power by prescribing morals here and there.

To prescribe is to judge, to put oneself in a higher position of authority, power. This is why moralisers are often perceived as nettlesome. Even if it seems *prima facie* that the morals are altruistic, the prescriber puts himself in a position where he can dictate what is to be done and believed. If enough heads agree with the ideology, the prescriber/preacher gains further power, eventually influencing standardised law. In relation, the followers of the creed become such followers as the creed offers them more power, even if it entails joining the group, the secular congregation. If one has a caring, compassionate character, one will be motivated to believe in a creed that objectifies it as true for all – humanism for example. This creed then justifies the character of the follower, and thus his advocation of the creed is in reality an advocation of himself, self-empowerment. Only a minority are able to empower themselves without needing to join a group, an ideology, a 'false consciousness', as even Marx's Engels put it.

Thus normative morality is a tool for power. The *modus operandi* of the minds of the majority is subconscious. Most people are completely unaware of why they believe in the creeds they do, be they religious or secular (in truth, religion and ideology are the same thing: unfounded belief systems). A priest most often actually believes what he preaches. Likewise, subjects think they know 'right from wrong', and this morality profoundly influences their actions, but hardly any can substantiate their beliefs. Ask someone why they believe that equality is good, why compassion should be extended to all, why revenge is to be avoided, why humility is a virtue, why happiness should be pursued, why everyone has natural rights – ask them and you will receive either a blank stare or 'nonsense on stilts'. But just as crusaders and missionaries paid dearly for their conscious beliefs, so today do those who put faith in human rights, animal rights, democracy, freedom, feminism, nationalism, justice, law, environmental ethics, capitalism, socialism, etc. All are, in the final analysis, as groundless as religion – they are in praxis religion – but all part of the human method of power play. The statement 'God exists' is as non-provable as the statement 'equality is good'.

Removing oneself from a moral ideology can be both liberating and denigrating, depending on one's strength of character. As above, joining a flock can offer protection, consolation and thus a form of empowerment;

leaving the flock can therefore be hazardous and inimical to one's interest. But to those trapped rather than protected within the fence of morality, basing actions on what one has been inculcated to believe to be proper, rather than what would most ensure one's advancement and development – to such a person the truth would set him free, as John the apostle expressed it. Only, opposed to that acolyte, here is true truth and free freedom. 'None are more hopelessly enslaved than those who falsely believe they are free' wrote a true *Freigeist*, Goethe.

To summarise, we must distinguish descriptive from prescriptive ethics; and human characteristics from values and vices. We can describe characteristics such as compassion and aggression, but we cannot prescribe them as values or vices unless we humans have a purpose. Without God there can be no absolute purpose, *telos*, as we were not made with such an end in mind. Therefore the general moral question, 'What ought we do?' is an invalid question, that can only be responded to with the question, '…if we want to achieve, What?' Without an if-clause (always ultimately based on subjective desire) as condition, there can be no ought-clause. As Schopenhauer stated, 'we shall not speak of an "unconditional ought", since this involves a contradiction … Generally, we shall not speak of "ought" at all, for we speak in this way to children and to peoples still in their infancy.' (*The World as Will and Representation*, §53.) An unconditioned (by an if-clause) ought is a contradiction because a means (an *ought*) necessarily implies an end (an *if*). Thus all moral prescriptions never express facts but really, often unwittingly, express the desire of one person or people to change the behaviour of another. Morality as such is power play.

The term 'moral progress' implies that there is an absolute standard towards which we are progressing. But this standard would be an ideal good, in the style of a Platonic Form or Divine decree, in other words this standard is a phantom of the mind, a delusion. It has no basis in reality. With regard to this ideal good standard, one can always ask, 'Good for what purpose?' – and again it is the purpose that is subjective, not objective: one being's preferred purpose will differ from another's, from peace and harmony to war and adventure. Morals do not progress or retrogress, because there can be no standard to judge them by. As in the rest of nature, there is only flux. We are not above the violence of the brutes because we know morality; rather, we are above the brutes because we use the violence that is 'morality'. The moral ideals of today will be viewed as immoral tomorrow, and so on *ad infinitum*. Pride, for instance, was considered the 'crown of the virtues' by Aristotle; but as the worst of the cardinal sins by medieval Christianity. One can only strive to perceive the show from above.

Law is Force

As soon as we are born, and oftentimes before, we are subject to laws of state to which we never gave consent. At least in Christianity today the forced adherence to the creed through infant baptism is later ceremoniously confirmed at the age of reason. In law, we are never asked to confirm our belief at the age of reason, or at any age whatever. It is enforced allegiance to other people's desired order. In the West, one can decide to reject a religion without much consequence. Apostasy and atheism in many Islamic states, however, is punishable by death. Indeed apostasy is declared a capital crime in the Koran and Hadiths. In nations where law is directly based on religion, apostasy is a rejection of law, and thus a grave offence as it threatens the belief system that sustains the power of the oligarchy – today the Ayatollahs and their politician cronies. When the Church in Europe was the predominant basis of law, apostasy was capital offence, despite the Commandment prohibiting killing. The Spanish Inquisition provides ample examples.

In the West such rejections of religion are no longer crimes. Though evidence of the former union of religion, morality and law can be witnessed, for example, in the United States of America – constitutionally secular but demographically Christian – where the word 'atheism' is frequently used as an insult, connoted with immorality and lawlessness. This is analogous to the Arabic Islamic word 'kafir', or infidel. Even blasphemy was only officially legalised in the United Kingdom in 2008. Such rejections and antagonisms towards religion are no longer crimes in the Enlightened non-Islamic states because the oligarchy, which creates and enforces law, is no longer ostensibly religious. The basis of law no longer depends on belief in God and His commandments and examples. In this age, the basis of law is theoretically based mostly on contractarianism, 'social contract theory', and utilitarianism. But as we saw above, contractarianism and utilitarianism are without objective ground, as those grounds are both unwittingly Christian and subjective desiderata – made to seem objective through twenty centuries of habitual creed.

'Theoretically based', I write. Law is practically based on the wish and whim of an 'elected' elect, and of those hidden puppet-masters who lobby and sponsor those elect, often for them to be elected. Democracy is another phantom that tricks the populace into believing they have power and freedom over their masters, now not so much the clergy as the financiers. Near half of the money one makes as a wage slave goes to the state via taxes, which then distributes the lucre to its collection bureaucracy and to banks, through interest-ridden loans, which are even originally created *ex nihilo*. Effectively most people spend a significant amount of time working for other people from whom they will derive little if no benefit, and this accounts in part for the wide differential between rich and poor. As the infamous Ragnar Redbeard put it, being able to vote for your tax-gatherers every fourth year does not make you free or powerful – it establishes you as slave.

Even if it were effectual, democracy is neither an objectively good institution. Plato argued against democracy as he considered it rule by a mob who are generally unwise and ignorant of their own interests. An aristocracy of Philosopher Kings did he prefer, thereby empowering himself – much like his student Aristotle who considered philosophising as the greatest intellectual virtue which brought Philosophers as close to human perfection as is possible. God Himself, for Aristotle, was a philosopher. Perfection is the complete attainment of something to its purpose, its if-clause – with no objective purpose, there is no perfection. Democracy is based on the principle of equality, a baseless though common idea. Western nations that criticise theocracies for not being democratic are often rebuked by the fair comment that the theocrats consider the decrees of their god to be above the decrees of their citizens: the Law of God has authority over the Law of Man.

Both theocracy and democracy, however, have hollow foundations. There is no correct resolution between the two as they are both false in the sense that one oligarchy is maintained through the illusion of religion, the other through the illusion of egalitarianism. Below the epidermis two power structures display threatening behaviour; words and arguments are the epiphenomena of the underlying struggle: force-on-force. Each side considers the other immoral, as decadent infidels or as undemocratic dogmatists. All is sophistry, language is but another evolved tool for power.

If one wants to live in an ordered society, a subjective if-clause itself, then one ought to advocate infrastructural laws, such as road law, property rights, technological research and manufacture, etc. One may do this if it is in one's interest. However, it may also be in one's interest to break these laws. The subjective clause then delivering contrary imperatives, oughts, to the first general subjective clause. It will often be retorted that if you want people to obey the law then you ought to also obey it, lest you be a hypocrite. However, this is an error, albeit a sometimes useful one.

The error lies in the fact that the if-clause does not logically imply the ought-clause, the end does not imply the given means. The hidden premise which would justify the conclusion that I ought to obey the law would be: 'people ought to have equal power'. The syllogism would then run: 'People ought to obey the law, (people ought to have equal power), therefore I ought to obey the law'. But this hidden premise is not objectively true. It comes from a subjective desire which not all people would share, especially not rulers. An example will highlight the mistake: If you want to eat chicken, you ought to let chickens eat you. The absurdity is here revealed – we do not, except for a minority of vegetarians, consider that chickens ought to have equal power to humans. However most people believe that all humans ought to have equal power. But equality is not an objective, prescriptive fact – it is only an objective descriptive fact in mathematics. The concept of hypocrisy is only meaningful if one considers that everyone ought to be equal. Without that false idol, hypocrisy is meaningless. It is not said of a King that he is a hypocrite because he does not wash his own dishes.

It is pure fact that breaking a law may be in your interest so long as you are not caught and punished. It may also be in your interest that this fact is not known by the majority as it could impede your own power. If one considers crimes such as theft and murder in a proto-society setting, we see that those with the real power will commit those acts (not 'crimes') not only without guilt but even with pride, as a trophy reflecting natural power. Might is right is *lex naturalis*. When a group seize power, the laws they set will serve to maintain that power. It will be in their interest to make the ruled populace servile by propagating within them false ideologies that hinder revolution (which would simply be another group seizing power) and which promote the ruling power base. The Protestant work ethic is an apt example; the Reformation itself an example of when a group seizes power from its masters – here from the Catholic Church who demanded taxes seemingly justified by their ideology. Even Marx noted that the law 'do not steal' is merely a method by which property-owning classes maintain power – in a communist nation without property such a law would not even be intelligible.

A state, a government, is only a group of individuals who tell others what can and cannot be done. If one disobeys these commands one is physically assaulted by the group's minions (the police and armed services). Only the state, at least in most of Europe, is permitted to use physical violence and weaponry, to all others this is forbidden. The Second Amendment of the United States Constitution protects a right to keep and bear arms, something denied to most Europeans. This makes an armed revolution more difficult in the vast peninsula of Eurasia, thereby empowering the state. 'Violence and aggression is wrong, unless performed on behalf of the state' – who really falls for such propaganda? The Catholic 'Just War Theory' is an analogous case: Thomas Aquinas argued that violence and murder are grave sins, unless committed for a 'just cause' which for him meant a Catholic cause. The Catholic Church still adheres to this theory. A state is a power structure that promotes law inside but war outside. It is in its essence a very large gang. Internal laws of harmony maintain its power, and external acts of violence advance its power. There is just a matter of degree between a biker gang and a nation. A gang within a nation may be labelled as outlaws, but a nation is as 'criminal' in its international efforts. Think only of war, arms trading, or drug distribution: the British, for example, used military might against the Chinese state to ensure their continued trade of opium to the Chinese – the Opium Wars of the nineteenth century. Today the sale of alcohol within Britain is considered, in this sense, 'criminal' to most Islamic states. There is no right or wrong about it though, only difference. (Against the notion that the Islamic states' prohibitions are wrong as they are based on a fictional character's (Allah's) prescription in the Koran, one merely states that a basis of non-prohibition in western states is based on the equally fictional notion that 'happiness is good'. Again, there are only value differences based on power structures entrenched within cultural histories.)

Into this state gang we are born, into its laws we are inculcated and subjected. If we want to live in an ordered society we would accept some laws. But many laws are injurious to those who are not cattle to be prod by bank clerks and milksop civil servants. Dignity is pride in one's own powers. A man with dignity will not accept gladly being continually observed by the state. The proliferation of video cameras on every street and street corner, inside every public building, is an affront to the dignity of men, as is any form of state surveillance. The argument that one has nothing to be concerned about if one has done nothing wrong is reprehensible. It assumes that what the state claims to be wrong is objectively wrong; and it assumes that the state is not corrupt in that it always works in one's service. Furthermore, being continually watched is a constant reminder that the state has power over you: it can watch you, but you cannot watch it. Despite the Englishman Orwell's warnings, the English have not shed their fleece.

When the people of northern Europe refused to pay tax to the Catholic Church and to follow their dogma, it was not in the end considered a crime but a great liberation, a victory for freedom. Martin Luther and Henry VIII are not considered criminals in their homelands because their refusal to obey the law could not be punished by force. Their own power was too great for the Catholic Church to oppress, though much blood was spilt until the Peace of Westphalia over a century later. The same crime, or liberation, occurred when the United States was stolen/liberated from the British crown in the year of Hume's death. When a number of people rob a bank it is considered a crime, when a number of people steal a country it is considered a great deed. Morality and law are mere symptoms of the underlying power base. As world and history reveal, moralities and laws are in constant flux as indicators of shifting power-plates operating underground. As Max Stirner noted, 'The state calls its own violence law, but that of the individual, crime.'

Infanticide, in our age a heinous 'crime', was not only in Sparta allegedly proper but in Mesoamerica, Ancient Egypt, Carthage and countless other cultures a religious rite. Homosexuality was a crime until the late 1960s in the United Kingdom. In the early 21st Century homophobia has reached the status of a crime. This change does not reflect moral progress or retrogress, but merely that an older Christian power base lost power to a new base, a form of Liberalism. Neither power base is objectively better or worse, they are mere competitors. Where the religion has not lost its stronghold, homosexuality is still considered a crime. 'Moral progress', again, assumes an objective moral code as standard to which we are moving – nonsense. Morals do not progress they change – analogous again to religions. It is also analogous to the paradigm shifts in science, emphasised by Thomas Kuhn. As well as a moral ideology, we also live in a scientific ideology which is still dominated by materialism. All these aspects of an ideology are interrelated: a materialist scientism aids a political creed striving against the former (non-materialist) Christian power structure. Law reflects power, not truth or justice. Thrasymachus and Callicles were straw-manned by Plato, Sophism was demoted as sophistry; but these pre-Socratic philosophers were never defeated in logic only power, the irony of which we now see. The Age of Pericles was the age that understood that man was the measure of all things.

Around our planet, abortion is both legal and illegal, to varying extents, depending on which power structure resides in which location. It is futile arguing whether or not abortion ought to be legal – there is no correct answer. Only power decides the outcome. Those powers will take whichever argument is in their interest. Not reason, but power decides ideology. Not only ideology but territory: the Romans did not use reasoned argument to gain lands for the Empire, but force. Brute expansion, the gain of power through land and its resources, has often required to be disguised as morality to a people who are necessarily indoctrinated into a moral code – the power elite use both ideology and military force to maintain and gain power, so the latter cannot be seen to contradict the former. Such disguises include the German term *Lebensraum* – living space – which was an expedient in particular to the later National Socialists. Likewise, Zionism was and is an expedient to certain

Jews. During the British Empire, expansion was clothed with the idea that bringing civility to barbarian nations was a moral imperative and as such the sole motive for thieving land. In more modern times, expansion is often cloaked as a moral imperative that brings peace, democracy and freedom to a country. This only works if one believes that peace, democracy and freedom are objective morals. If one denies that, one denies excuses for expansion. But of course, that does not make expansion 'immoral', it makes it simply a fact of nature and history. In a nation where theft is not a vice, the nation's expansion – theft of land – would not need to be disguised under moral clothing. In a capitalist state where property is sacred, and so where theft is a cardinal sin, the gain of substantial property as land must be masked – masked by those engaged in *realpolitik*. We are mostly prisoners locked in a cave, putting faith in the reality of shadows cast before us.

Life is Will to Power

The history of man is the history of war interspersed with periods of rest. It is commonly believed that the will to survive is the predominant urge of every organism, and that the will to power is an immoral usurpation. But as morality and immorality are fictions, the will to power is set free from condemnation, and also thereby in request of a new explanation. Everything that lives instinctually seeks power, survival is merely the lowest degree of that drive to power: one cannot gain power if one is not alive to do so. Thus does Nietzsche assimilate the will to survive into the will to power. All morality, all law, all ideology, are merely expressions of this primal drive. Once that is understood, the gates of perception are opened upon a dawn of light – a light that vanquishes the guilt from ambition and pride, indeed conduces their blossom. In this final section we shall come to understand the origin and meaning of the *Wille zur Macht*, an understanding that sanctions power as the principle of all life. Understanding power empowers.

Despite calling Kant a 'deformed concept cripple', Nietzsche can be seen as a neo-Kantian. In fact, only in this light can Nietzsche be properly understood as he began his philosophical profession as a disciple of Schopenhauer, a self-labeled apostle of Kant. Despite Nietzsche's later rejection of Schopenhauer, the rejection was only in part. Schopenhauer's notion of the will was not rejected by Nietzsche, it was merely reassessed optimistically, and Schopenhauer's will originates in Kant's Transcendental Idealism.

It is said that Kant brought about the Copernican revolution in Philosophy. In his later years, during the Enlightenment, Kant wrote his *magnum opus*, 'The Critique of Pure Reason'. He argued that the world we perceive is mostly our own creation. Before him John Locke and others (including Democritus twenty-five centuries ago, and Galileo) had reasoned that colours, sounds, smells and all other qualia exist only ideally – as idea. The blue of the sky existed not up there but only in here, in the mind, as a translation of light waves into a sensation, colour. The sound of a falling tree exists only in minds, external to that mind no sound exists, only air waves to be potentially translated. Reality-out-there, and reality-in-here were not identical. Each animal translates the external reality according to the structures, the forms, of its mind. Reality is in this sense created by the mind. A bee sees ultraviolet light, a human does not – as a result the floral world, the same externally, differs internally. Locke called internal sensations 'secondary qualities' (colours, etc.) and external things (solid three-dimensional objects) and their movements and number 'primary qualities'. The former change according to mind type, the latter remain the same.

Kant extended the scope of secondary qualities, thereby almost eliminating the primary. What was revolutionary in Kant's philosophy was that he found not only the sensations corresponding to the senses as created by our mind, but also created were space and time and twelve other forms of the understanding. Space and time, in other words, do not exist 'out there' but are merely ways in which we translate reality according to our minds' inherent structure. Other types of mind will perceive the world in other spatio-temporal orders, if not other non-spatio-temporal orders. A fly, for instance, experiences time differently from a human, much to our irritation. Altering human minds' operational structure with psychedelic compounds results in a distortion of time and space. These distortions are not necessarily hallucinations but the breaking down of ordinary functioning, ordinary consciousness. Space and time do not exist really, but only ideally, thus the term Idealism. The world that we perceive Kant labels 'phenomena'. The world that exists independent of any mind translation he calls 'noumena': the universe-in-itself, not in us. Thus did Schopenhauer write, 'Before Kant we were in time; now time is in us.'

Whilst being in general agreement with Kant's Idealism, Schopenhauer qualified the doctrine. For Kant the 'thing-in-itself' (beyond our representation of it) is unknowable in principle as knowing involves perception, but we cannot perceive the thing-in-itself because perception is substantially creation of the phenomena. Analogously, we cannot see a pitch-dark room as seeing involves lighting. So for Kant we can only understand that the thing-in-itself exists as such, we cannot possibly know what it is. Schopenhauer here interjected that there is one thing-in-itself that we can know, and that is our will. Our inner self, beyond our psychological self-conceptions based on language, is the force that is the individual. This force, this will, is that which forms representations of all other forces – for humans this will represents other forces as qualitative three-dimensional objects in time. Even our own bodies are representations according to the forms of spatio-temporal representation. It is very important to note that the body does not contain the force, rather the body is the force, represented according to the structure of our mind. It is not Dualism (spirit and body) but Idealism. Materialism is the world as representation. The materialist view leads to Dualism as it fails to explain, for instance, how consciousness can emerge from material objects. This failure indicates that consciousness must be separate then from matter, the brain, etc., thence the 'spirit' is concocted as antidote. But both Materialism and Dualism stem from conflating the representation of the world for the world-in-itself. Once one understands that the world is representation, one understands that that which represents the world according to its forms cannot itself exist solely as a representation. What represents *representations*, as it were, is what Schopenhauer calls the *will*. Hence his masterpiece is entitled *The World as Will and Representation*.

For Schopenhauer, not only humans but animals too have their own wills that fashion their world according to their own particular forms of representation. The represented world becomes a simpler place as one goes down the hierarchy of complexity of organisms – an ant's worldview will not be the complex myriad that we experience. Descending further, even plants represent the world, but in a relatively primitive manner, focusing primarily on light. For Schopenhauer, the descent traverses all of that which exists. One terminates with inorganic matter whose will is gravity. A star has no consciousness as we understand it, no intelligence nor memory – so its will is basic, but powerful nonetheless. Force does not act on dead matter; matter is a representation of force from the human perspective. Matter and force is essentially the same thing, the former our representation of that thing which is a will-in-itself (not 'free will'). Idealism resolves the problems of Materialism and Dualism.

However, as space and time are forms of our representation, and as separation is only possible in terms of spatial and temporal division, Schopenhauer understands that in reality all is one. In reality there is neither time nor space – a noumenal reality perhaps glimpsed by Aldous Huxley amongst a multitude of other pyschonauts and mystics. This unity is the basis of Schopenhauer's ethical theory. He believes that the perpetual striving of each apparent force is futile as once an end is achieved it loses its allure and so we then suffer boredom or a further craving. If we do not achieve an end, misery also follows. Thus every force always results in wanting, boredom or disappointment. For this reason is Schopenhauer known as a pessimist. For the same reason Schopenhauer suggests the ascetic path of life, shunning desire as it only can lead to suffering. Despite being highly critical of Christianity and other religions, the monastic lifestyle is promoted. For Schopenhauer being ethical means the rejection of selfishness and acting to advance the true unity of which we are all an aspect. Schopenhauer's ethical theory, it is vital to recall, is descriptive not prescriptive; he writes of states of character that can be called ethical according to the interpretation of his ontology – he understands that talk of *oughts* is infantile error, as quoted above.

Friedrich Nietzsche can be considered Schopenhauer's successor. Born into the middle of the Nineteenth Century, Nietzsche became Professor of Philology in his mid-twenties as well as becoming officially stateless. He had rejected religion prior to that, having read Schopenhauer. His first philosophical writings presupposed a complete Schopenhauerian evaluation of a Schopenhauerian ontology. Nietzsche's later works reject the evaluation but not the fundamental ontology. For Nietzsche the striving of the will was not to be devalued as it led to suffering – as suffering was not objectively 'bad'. To believe it was, as did Schopenhauer, was to assume a slavish perspective on life, a perspective in the West established by the error and corruption that was Christianity. Logically, the if-clause of desiring the abolition of suffering is not objective. Suffering can strengthen, empower – and for Nietzsche power is the fundamental end of life, not happiness. Happiness is merely the temporary side-effect of overcoming an obstacle, that is, of gaining power thereover. To those who are not powerful enough to overcome a challenge, their low-grade happiness stagnates as mere tranquillity. As illustration, compare the heaven of Christianity – originally a cult for the weak – with the heaven of the mighty Vikings: that is, a heaven of peace and calm opposed to a heaven where battle commences each day.

Happiness represented as ideals in the afterlife is conditioned by the strength of the evaluators.

Therefore Nietzsche takes Schopenhauer's *will to survive* and renames it the *will to power*, essentially re-evaluating striving in a positive light, but also extending striving beyond survival to empowerment. Everything wills power, though most often unconsciously. A plant strives for root and sun space, but it has no consciousness about the matter. The will to power is essentially the plant, in fact all 'life is will to power'. The will to power means then growth, development, advance; not necessarily conscious greed though that is another form of it. Moreover, the will to power is the inner will of things, 'things' being the mere representation of other wills according to the perspective of another will – as in Schopenhauer's Idealism.

The will to survive is the lowest expression of the will to power, the will to truth is a higher form of the will to power. Seeking truth is a means to the seeking of power, it is not a drive in itself. The more information an organism has over its surroundings, the more power has it to survive predators or track prey. The will to truth in less complex organisms is manifested as merely sense organs, as a means to the will to power, and in higher organisms also as memory, concept formation, rationality, curiosity. All of these faculties are part of the armory that is the will to power. Life does not contain the will to power, life is the will to power, its systematic force – it is a rewording of 'life' rather than the imposition of an élan vital. All scientific progress is a means to empower a people, sometimes to the detriment of other peoples, as the advancement of weaponry reveals. In higher organisms, truth often provides less power than falsity. If a person or group gain more power through false propaganda, then so be it. The end is power, not truth. But an enemy knowing the falsity that lies at the heart of their adversary has thereby acquired their Achilles' Heel, though the shot may still be difficult. Humans most often prefer to maintain their illusions than accept refutations, as the refutation frequently is not only of a person's belief, but of his entire identity, stability and way of life. Force and rhetoric commonly trump reasoned argument – a badly-kept secret famously expressed by Emperor Nero's tutor and advisor, Seneca: 'Religion is regarded by the common people as true, by the wise as false, and by the rulers as useful.'

For Nietzsche power is a universal drive, but not one that could resolve Hume's Guillotine thus delivering objective prescriptions. The if-clause would here be 'if I (or my group) am to attain power' – but the ought-clause derived therefrom could not be universal as what one person or group ought to do to attain power is often the precise contrary to what other people ought to do in order to gain power. So no universal prescriptive morality can be derived from the will to power as universal principle. Nero's means, ought-clause, of attaining power would not be happily accepted by his Christian or slum-dwelling subjects. Napoleon's means to his end were not his enemies' means. Although the end of power is objective, the means are subjective, so the is-ought gap is not bridged here, nor is it desired to be bridged.

Nietzsche contends that the objective morality that most western subjects put faith in today germinated two millennia ago with the advent of Christianity. When the Jews became subject to Roman rule, their means of overcoming that curtailment of power was the revaluation of Roman values, a revaluation that became the dominant religion of the world. Roman values were an example of what Nietzsche named 'master morality': a system that held characteristics such as strength, honour, pride, courage, fortitude, etc., as the highest of values. A cult emerged which completely inversed master morality. It was a cult which preached weakness, humility, compassion, faith, hope and charity to be the highest virtues. Such characteristics of course empowered the weak – those who needed charity, hope, equality, compassion given to them, a God who blessed them as being weak. A weakling who has nothing to be proud of will gain power by proliferating the view that humility is a virtue, pride a vice. 'Blessed are the meek: for they shall inherit the earth' Jesus said, Matthew reported. This kind of ideology that empowers and ennobles the weak for being weak Nietzsche calls 'slave morality'. It is weakness and mediocrity dressed as virtue. This inverted ideology quickly spread, despite the Roman criminalisation of it. Almost three centuries after Jesus' alleged resurrection, Constantine legalised and converted to Christianity. Soon thereafter the Roman Empire fell. This slave morality has now spread to two billion adherents after two millennia.

Moreover, so ingrained in our culture is Christianity that the vast majority of those who proclaim their atheism still accept Christian morality as the only type of morality, as 'common sense', without acknowledging that it is only one type of morality: Christian slave morality. Nietzsche's later aim was to offer a new morality by revealing the Achilles' Heel of the old. 'God is dead' means that if one no longer believes in God, one no longer has any justification for Christian morality. This for two main grounds. Firstly, the imperatives given in the Bible cannot be said to be revealed as objective by an omnipotent, omniscient God as He does not exist. Secondly, if we were not created by God, in His image, in His likeness, then we have no objective purpose. As mentioned, only an artefact designed with a purpose in mind, such as a knife, can have a purpose. If we were not designed, we are free from purpose and thus free from any derived if clauses.

Our freedom as such was a tenet of the existentialists in the twentieth century. However, more often than not, they still tried to devise normative ethics, and thereby failed. The consequences of atheism were too powerful for even these self-proclaimed free thinkers. Theoretical nihilism is the consequence of atheism, not existentialism, humanism, utilitarianism, contractarianism – not even socialism. Socialists believe in egalitarianism: that everyone ought to be equal. This ought has no objective condition (if-clause), and this belief is not universal but, writes Nietzsche, a legacy of the Christian morality – that all are equal under the eyes of God. Even Anarchists who are vehemently against faith still retain faith in Christian values in their egalitarianism. Although Karl Marx called himself a 'scientific socialist', describing what would happen rather than what should happen – and thus avoiding the accusation of being prescriptive – his later brethren and comrades were and are not. In reality, despite his plea, he was prescriptive: 'Workers of the World, unite!' is an imperative, a prescription, not a description. Lenin's reworking of the motto further exposes its slave religious origin: 'Workers and Oppressed Peoples and Nations of the World, Unite!' Lenin himself thereby using illusion to gain power, an illusion perhaps even believed by him; power works almost entirely behind the veil of consciousness. The priestly class exploit oppression to gain and maintain power, their congregation exploiting the slave illusion for their own power – the common symbiosis of delusion. This is often not a conscious deception; priests and their people actually believe the obviously false content of their religion despite its lack of proof, its contradictions, its variation through history. Power decides, not reason.

Extracting oneself from this symbiotic relationship may result in lost power if one has not the resolve and strength to be an individual. Being able to rely on one's own judgement of what is valuable to oneself is not possible for the greater population of the earth. What is a value to another may not be a value to oneself, as objective morality is illusion: neo-nihilism. A reason for the prefix 'neo-' in neo-nihilism is that traditional nihilism often denies the existence of 'truth'. That last clause *prima facie* bites its own tail as it is a truth that claims there is no truth. Nietzsche did claim there was no truth – thus his perspectivist tag – but he meant this in the sense of the denial of objective morals: values are conditioned by the subject, or by they to whom one is subject. It is merely a semantic issue, as if one extends the denial of truth to Nietzsche's philosophy, that too becomes not a truth but a perspective. But if one believes that it is true that all is perspective, one concurs with Nietzsche implying that his philosophy is truth. Neo-nihilism thus limits the definition of perspectivism and so accepts certain types of truth, *viz.* those formed and aligned according to the structure of the mind rather than according to a created structure of immanent reality.

It is important to note the distinction between theoretical nihilism and practical nihilism. This distinction is, in fact, the main cause of the label 'neo-nihilism' that I have applied to the thought of this text. Theoretical nihilism is the view that there exist no objective values. Practical nihilism is the view that there exist no values at all. Thus neo-nihilism does not reject the existence of values, it only rejects the existence of objective values. Indeed, living is valuating. One can value food when hungry, one can value beauty, one can value friends – one can value violence and one can value peace. Even perception itself is a form of valuation: one perceives what can be beneficial *vis-à-vis* power. We do not directly perceive radio waves as these were not beneficial in our evolutionary past. One values what is in one's power interest. Those with more power will value things that increase their power, such as valour, an enemy to test oneself against, courage, fortitude, intellect, influence. Those with less strength will value things such as humility, civility, servitude, submission, an eternal afterlife of peace, etc. Master morality and slave morality are different valuations conditioned by different typologies. Often one is conditioned to value things that are not in one's interest (but the Church or state's interest) – thus does neo-nihilism break bonds: it destroys old values to enable the creation of values new.

All is force, all is energy, all is will to power. You are will to power. You are born into a world of competing powers, they compete for your adherence as neighbouring planets compete for equidistant meteorites. If you have not the inherent will to fight the powers, you will join them thereby augmenting their power. But if you stand apart, deflecting external imperatives, refusing submission to any god, creed, state, law or ideology, never surrendering your will to the will of others – if such a stance you take, apotheosis to a heavenly body will you manifest: Yes, as Nietzsche decreed, 'The free man is a warrior.'

VIII

The Teutonic Shift
from Christian Morality:
Kant- Schopenhauer – Nietzsche

Introduction

- This talk aims to trace the decline of Christian morality from the perspective of three influential German thinkers, a fall which according to Nietzsche has still not been accomplished – in the West we still unwittingly abide by a Christian ethic.
- It may be considered odd that I do not include Germans such as Feuerbach or Marx, but this is because the most radical break from Christian morality is achieved in Nietzsche, and he inherits the philosophy of Schopenhauer and thus ultimately Kant.
- I shall present this lineage by considering for each philosopher both his ethical theory and his ontological theory, as they are in each case intertwined and necessary for an understanding of the subsequent thinker. But we shall begin with some historical context:

Immanuel Kant (1724 – 1804)

- Born in Königsberg, Prussia. The capital of Prussia till 1700 when Berlin capitalised. (Now Kaliningrad, an enclave of Russia in Europe.)
- Born into a family of harness-makers.
- Kant's family were *Pietists*, a branch of Lutheran Christianity that was in conflict with the orthodox Lutheranism of Prussia.
  - Frederick the Great (king from 1740 to 1786) utilised Pietism to push his reform past the established aristocracy who were predominantly orthodox Lutheran.

- Thus from the beginning Kant was immersed in religious conflicts, including the aftermath of the *Thirty Years' War* (1618–1648) between the Catholics and the Protestants.
- These religious antagonisms affected academia with philosophers such as the Leibnizian philosopher Christian Wolff being ousted from the University of Halle (1723) because his views on pre-established harmony diverged from Pietist views on free will!
  o To call oneself a Spinozist was akin to calling oneself a Fascist today.
- But when Frederick the Great took the throne (1740), freedom of thought became tolerated and even encouraged.
- This was a catalyst to the whole Enlightenment, where thinking was freeing itself from the chains of specific religions.
- When Frederick the Great died, his nephew Frederick William II took over and immediately tried to restrict free thought, partly due to his Rosicrucian (Lutheran secret cult linked to the Stone Masons) cronies.
  o He (via Wöllner) sent Kant a letter threatening him for perceived irreligiosity, which curtailed Kant's publications until the king's death in 1797.
- Kant was not religious though he did have faith in an abstract god. He was alleged of atheism many a time.
- He was known as the 'all-crusher' as he crushed the traditional arguments for the existence of God, and he crushed the extent of possible knowledge.
- For Kant, the purpose of religion was morality.
- But morality could not be based on religion as this inevitably led to conflict, in terms of the subjective interpretations of the religion.
  o *Instead, in order to stop the possibility of these conflicts, morality would have to be based on reason, as reason is deemed universal and thus delivers universal conclusions (as in mathematics and logic).*

Kant's Moral Theory

- Kant's theory of morality is called *deontology* meaning duty-ology.
- It is chiefly contained in three works:

- o   *The Groundwork of a Metaphysics of Morals* (GMM)
- o   *The Critique of Practical Reason* (CPcR)
- o   *The Metaphysics of Morals* (MM)
- In outline, Kant argues that one ought to act upon intentions that are not based on one's feelings but on one's reason, the latter of which dictates that one should do that which one could will to become a universal law.
  - o   i.e. feelings or consequences are irrelevant for being moral.
  - o   Shopkeeper example: a shopkeeper who returns the correct change to a child is only moral if he does it not for long-term gain but only for duty.
    - ▪ For a utilitarian, concerned with consequences, the intention is irrelevant – in contradistinction.
- Kant seeks to prove this 'supreme principle of morality' in the GMM.
  - o   He begins with an assumption of *natural teleology*: that every organ and faculty in a body has a purpose (*telos*).
  - o   If the function of a human were happiness (as many Greek philosophers believed) then the faculty of Reason would have no purpose/*telos*, as instinct would suffice for this end (as in animals).
  - o   Therefore, Reason's *telos* cannot be one's own happiness (egoism), but rather a 'good will' (altruism).
  - o   Therefore one ought to act from a good will, which is one's duty.
  - o   The duty of a good will is formalised by Kant as the *Categorical Imperative*:
    - ▪ "I ought never to act except in such a way that I can also will that my maxim should become a universal law."
      - • This is the first formulation.
      - • It therefore prohibits lying, breaking promises, etc.
  - o   There are two more chief formulations of the Categorical Imperative which flow from the first, Kant argues:
    - ▪ *The Formula of the End in Itself*:
      - • "Act in such a way that you always treat humanity, whether in your own person or in the person of any other, never

          simply as a means, but always at the same time as an end."

- *The Formula of Kingdom-of-Ends*:
  - "So act as if you were through your maxims a law-making member of a kingdom of ends."
- (Also important is *The Formula of the Law of Nature*:)
  - "Act as if the maxim of your action were to become through your will a universal law of nature."
    - This prohibits suicide and sexual 'perversions'.
      (This formula can be conflated for the first.)

- Moral statements for Kant must take the form of *Categorical Imperatives* (i.e. imperatives *without* an if-clause), they cannot take the form of *Hypothetical Imperative* (i.e. imperatives *with* an if-clause) as this would make all principles dependent on that non-rational if-clause:
  - E.g. "I ought not to steal, *if I don't want to feel guilty.*"
    - Such *hypothetical imperatives* are always based on egoistical desires and so never moral as they cannot be objective (only subjective).
  - (David Hume had argued that all ought-clauses come from if-clauses, and therefore ultimately all morality is based on subjective sentiment, never objective reason.)
- In sum, if morality is to be possible, it must be based on Reason, not on feeling or on consequence.
- Furthermore, Kant argues that if morality is to be possible we must postulate/assume three conditions:
  - *Free Will*
  - *Immortality of the Soul*
  - *God*
- These postulates are rather surprising, as he had previously crushed all previous arguments for God. He had also argued that the world was deterministic, thereby not allowing for free will.
  - But nonetheless, in the CPcR (and elsewhere), Kant points out that if we are not *free* to choose our actions, then morality is not possible.

- Without free will one could not be subject to praise or blame, and any *oughts* or duties would be meaningless maxims without efficacy.

o The *immortality of the soul* is postulated (but not 'proved') because:

- In striving to be moral, we strive for the happiness of all, including ourselves. Therefore we ought to become happy even if we do not achieve it in this lifetime. Thus because 'nature' gives us a *telos* that is not fully achievable, we must assume it will be achieved *ad infinitum*. (An *ought* here implies a 'can'.)

o *God* is postulated because:

- Happiness is when our will is in harmony with our environment. But as moral beings we ought to achieve happiness, though we cannot bring about the harmony of our environment with ourselves. But as such harmony ought to be achieved, we must postulate God the only omnipotent being Who could bring this about.

- "we ought to seek to further the highest good (hence this good must, after all, be possible). Therefore the existence of a cause of nature as a whole, distinct from nature ... is also postulated ... i.e. God." (CPcR, 125)

– Therefore, for Kant, morality leads to religion; religion does not lead to morality.

o Though, he is keen to point out, one cannot act for the sake of happiness or fellowship with God as this would then render one's action a hypothetical imperative and thus egoistic and amoral.

So although Kant begins the shift from Christian morality, dislodging its sanction from scripture and revelation to Reason, he nonetheless does not completely escape Christian assumptions.

—

In order to properly understand Schopenhauer's critique of Kant's deontology, and Schopenhauer's own further shift we must first examine Kant's ontology (theory of existence).

Kant's Ontology ('Transcendental Idealism')

- Kant's fame comes from his ontology: 'the Copernican Revolution in Philosophy', as it is known.
    o Transcendental Idealism is the notion that the world we perceive is mostly a creation of our minds, in a way far more radical than the empiricists saw it (e.g. Locke's Primary and Secondary Quality dichotomy) – but less radical than the Subjective Idealism of Berkeley.
    o As Einstein wrote:
        ▪ "I did not grow up in the Kantian tradition, but came to understand the truly valuable which is to be found in his doctrine … only quite late. It is contained in the sentence: 'The real is not given to us, but put to us (by way of a riddle).'"
    o In fact, as Werner Heisenberg added:
        ▪ "Einstein has not – as you sometimes hear – given the lie to Kant's deep thoughts on the idealization of space and time; he has, on the contrary, made a large step towards its accomplishment."
- Democritus, Galileo, Bacon and Locke (amongst others) had shown that 'secondary qualities' (colour, sound, taste, etc) do not exist in physical reality but are only mental interpretations of that reality.
- Kant went further and argued that even space, time, causality and a number of other categories, were also merely idea – or 'ideal' – not 'real' (thus "idealism").
    o In fact, these forms of the mind make experience/perception as such possible.
        ▪ They are conditions for the possibility of experience of the physical world.
            • They thus 'transcend' the physical world.
            • E.g. we do not get the idea of space from perception (as empiricists argued) because if we did not first map out

sensations into three-dimensional space, we would not perceive it *as* space.

  o   i.e. space is known before experience, indeed it makes experience as such possible.

- Further, just as we have no reason to assume that colours, sounds, etc., exist in physical reality, so neither do we have a reason to assume that space, time, etc., exist in reality.
- Thus 'reality' consists of two realms:
  o   *Phenomena* (our spatio-temporal qualitative world) and
  o   *Noumena* (the world in itself, independent of mental translation).

This limits our knowledge as we can never know the world as it is in itself, we always experience a mere appearance of the world which does not resemble it.

- Regarding morality, we can now understand that the three postulates (God, immortality, free will) are all possible even though they are unprovable:
  o   Each of us is a body in space and time, but we have an unknown existence that is noumenal ('pure apperception') (because knowing means translating to phenomena).
    ▪   As causality (determinism) is a category we project onto the world to make the world experiential, it does not exist noumenally. Therefore our ultimate noumenal selves can be *free* not caused, determined.
  o   Immortality and God, though absolutely unprovable, are at least possible. And as the conditions for morality, we should put our faith in them.
    ▪   As Kant famously wrote, "I had to deny knowledge in order to make room for faith" (CPR, preface).

Arthur Schopenhauer (1788 – 1860)

- Born in Danzig/Gdansk to wealthy merchant parents. Moved to Hamburg in 1793.
- In 1820 he became a lecturer at Berlin University concomitantly with Hegel, whom he considered a charlatan and state-sponsored sophist.

Schopenhauer mostly accepts Kant's ontology but refutes his deontology:

Criticism of Kant's Deontology

- For Kant, normativity (prescriptive ethics) is simply assumed and never proved.
    - "Kant's first false statement lies in his concept of ethics itself, a concept which we find articulated most clearly [in MM, p62]: 'In a practical philosophy it is not a concern to indicate reasons for what happens, but laws for what ought to happen, even if it never happens.' – This is already a decided *petitio principii* [question begging]. Who told you that there are laws to which we ought to subject our actions? Who told you that something ought to happen that never happens? – What justifies your assuming this beforehand and thereupon immediately to press upon us an ethics in a legislative-imperative form as the only possible sort?" (*On the Basis of Morals*, §4)
    - i.e. Kant assumes that morality must be prescriptive and thereafter seeks the conditions for this prescriptivity. He thus assumes what he seeks to prove: moral laws.
    - Furthermore, Schopenhauer identifies the origin of this unproved assumption as Judeo-Christian:
        - "I recognise no other source than the Decalogue [Ten Commandments, Exodus 20]. In general, in the centuries of Christianity, philosophical ethics has unconsciously taken its form from the theological. Since this ethics is now essentially dictatorial, the philosophical too, has appeared in the form of prescription and the doctrine of duty in all innocence and without suspecting that for this, first a further authority is necessary [God]. Instead, it supposes that this is its own and natural form." (*ibid.*)
        - Anticipating Nietzsche, Schopenhauer clearly considers Kant's allegedly rational morality to have religious groundings after all, despite Kant's attempt to unfetter it.

- The ultimate justification for such normativity is God. And so if 'God is dead', then this imperative form of morality is unjustified.
- Nietzsche's thought is further revealed as Schopenhauerian when we read in the same essay, in response to a Kantian imperative, "What slavish morals! ... slavish fear of the gods" (*ibid.*).
- Schopenhauer also criticises Kant by arguing that an unconditioned *ought* (an *ought* with no if-clause) is a contradiction in terms.
    o Every *ought* only has meaning ultimately in relation to threatened punishment or promised reward.
    o i.e. "I ought to do x, if I want (reward or no punishment)".
    o Hence, all *oughts* are *hypothetical* (with Hume) by definition.
    o Schopenhauer states that in fact this reward does sneak in the 'obscure' chapters on the postulates of morality: happiness and immortality.
- That which motivates a person to seek a rationally-grounded basis of morality is a non-rational desire/incentive.
    o Which for Kant was to emasculate religious (and political) authority.
    o Reason alone, Schopenhauer states, cannot motivate to action; reason is employed by desire/the will.
    o Therefore Kant's deontology cannot be based on reason but ultimately desire. Kant therefore fails his project.
- Free Will is impossible. Therefore instead of postulating it as necessary for morality, Kant should rather reject (normative) morality, as its condition (freedom) is impossible.
    o Schopenhauer wrote an essay on the freedom of the will. To quote Einstein once more, "I do not believe in free will. Schopenhauer's words: 'Man can do what he wants, but he cannot will what he wants' accompany me in all situations throughout my life and reconcile me with the actions of others, even if they are rather painful to me. This awareness of the lack of free will keeps me from taking myself and my fellow men too seriously as acting and deciding individuals, and from losing my temper."
- Briefly, Schopenhauer argues against free will thus:
    o One cannot consciously determine what one wishes.
    o Imagining an action is not the cause of an action.
    o The purpose of reason is to offer motives to the will, Reason itself does not cause actions. It is advisor, not executor.

- o   All phenomena are subject to causality as this is *a priori*.
- o   Schopenhauer uses the 'Water Analogy': water can wave, swirl, gush, etc., but is not thereby free.

Schopenhauer's Ontology

- –   Schopenhauer endorses the Kantian dichotomy of Phenomena and Noumena, but qualifies it thus:
  - o   All phenomena are our Representation of 'things-in-themselves' (as it were), represented by the cognitive filter of *merely* space, time and causality.
    - ▪   i.e. 'matter' and 'force' are but human representations of reality.
- –   But, further unlike Kant, Schopenhauer argued that we do also have a window unto this 'reality': our own 'will' (a term more akin to desire than to free will).
  - o   i.e. we have, in fact, two means of knowledge: *double-aspect theory:*
    - ▪   3rd-person knowledge (Representation)
    - ▪   1st-person knowledge (Will)
- –   Matter is the human representation of internal will.
  - o   Only in ourselves individually do we access both.
  - o   Even in other people, we only represent their will as body, and presuppose (by analogy) their will (see 'The Problem of Other Minds').
- –   The whole world is Will (energy with intent) and Representation of this will by other wills.
- –   Thus the name of his *magnum opus, 'The World as Will and Representation'*.
- –   Consequently, will does not emerge from matter, but rather matter is merely representation of will.
  - o   Thus materialism is false.
    - ▪   The 'forces' that are/act on matter are occult, to the materialist himself.
  - o   Dualism (soul/mind and matter) is also false as it endorses materialism and then tags on a spiritual substance to account for mind-matter interaction problems.
    - ▪   Dualism is the general Christian view.
- –   In sum, all matter-energy has an internal will that we represent as matter-energy.

– Basic, primal consciousness does not emerge from matter, 'matter' already has/is primal consciousness (will).

Schopenhauer's Moral Theory

– Having demolished Kant's moral theory, Schopenhauer now seeks to found his own.
  o As there are no *oughts*, Schopenhauer's theory is descriptive not prescriptive (normative).
    ▪ So the question is not whether an action ought to be done or not; but whether a person and his action are (descriptively) moral or not.
– One could, he writes, take a skeptical view and consider all morality to be mere control mechanism (anticipating Nietzsche once more).
– But one could only do this if one considered only egoism and malice as that which motivated people.
– Opposed to egoism and malice, compassion can be posited as a motivator.
  o But as compassion as incentive can only be known as 1st-person knowledge, it cannot be proved empirically.
    ▪ One can only know this if one has it oneself or on faith:
    ▪ Schopenhauer gives this example:
      • "[To believe that] Arnold von Winkelreid, as he cried out: 'Comrades true and loyal, care for my wife and child,' and embraced as many of the enemy spears as he could seize–therein had a self-interested intention; let him think so who can; I cannot do it ... should anyone still insist upon denying me the existence of all such [compassionate] actions, then, according to him, morals would be a science without a real object, like astrology and alchemy, and it would be a waste of time further to dispute about its basis. With him, therefore, I am at an end, and I speak to those who will admit the reality of the matter." – *On the Basis of Morals*

- Christianity is commendable in that it has placed compassion as a virtue in Europe (as it was not for the Greeks or Romans).
  - Yet it is predated by Hinduism.
  - Moreover, the list of Christian atrocities annuls this import.
- Compassion is possible as motive as it is an intuition of reality at its deepest level:
  - As space and time are ideal not real, and as individuation/ separation can only occur in space and/or in time, in ultimate reality all is one.
    - "That art thou", as it is said in Hinduism.
  - This is the basis of ethics: the intuition of ultimate reality.
  - Those living in the 'Veil of Maya' (space and time) are thus more prone to egoism (and malice).

Friedrich Nietzsche (1844 – 1900)

- Born in Röcken, near Leipzig, in Prussia.
- His father (a Lutheran pastor) died in 1849, and Nietzsche subsequently lived with his mother, grandmother, two aunts and younger sister.
- 1864: Studied Theology and Philology at University of Bonn but after one semester dropped theology as he had lost his faith.
- 1869: at the age of 24, Nietzsche became professor of Philology at the University of Basel, where he renounced his Prussian citizenship and was thereafter officially stateless for the rest of his life.

Nietzsche's Ontology

- Nietzsche endorsed Schopenhauer's general ideas about will and representation.
- But he revaluated and renamed the will:
  - Instead of the inner will, which is ultimately the immanence of everything, being the 'will to survive' (as Schopenhauer thought it), Nietzsche qualified it as the 'will to power'.
    - An organism does not merely strive for survival but for growth, development, power (most often unconsciously).
    - The will to survive is but the lowest degree of the

will to power, not a separate drive.
- ■ 'Value', for Nietzsche, is a matter of perspective: what brings a living system (or a power structure) more power.
- o All life is therefore evaluating and exploiting, in hierarchical degrees of systematisation.

Nietzsche's Moral Theory

- Nietzsche asked, *What is the value of compassion?*
- He cites Plato, Spinoza, La Rochefoucauld, Kant and various cultures throughout history as not valuing compassion.
  - o "[T]he issue was the value of the unegoistic, of the instincts of compassion, self-denial, self-sacrifice, precisely the instincts that Schopenhauer had gilded, deified, and made otherworldly until finally they alone were left for him as the 'values in themselves,' on the basis of which he said 'no' to life …This problem of the value of compassion and of the morality of compassion appears at first only as an isolated matter … Let us speak it aloud, this new challenge: we need a critique of moral values, for once the value of these values must itself be called into question … One has taken the value of these 'values' as given, as a fact …. What if the opposite were true? What if a symptom of regression lay in the 'good', likewise a danger … So that precisely morality would be to blame if a highest power and splendour of the human type – in itself possible – were never attained? So that precisely morality were the danger of dangers?" – *On the Genealogy of Morality*, Preface
- Nietzsche argued that one cannot simply, as did Schopenhauer, presuppose that compassion was the ground and identity of morality.
  - o Much like Schopenhauer chastising Kant for presupposing normativity.
  - o Etymologically the moral words of today do not derive from compassion.
    - ■ E.g. 'Good', from the German 'Gut' derives, he claims, from the Goths, and originally from their noble class.

- Nietzsche contends that the reason compassion is considered as almost synonymous with morality today is because of the power structure that is Christianity:
  - This structure began with the *Slave Revolt in Morals*:
    - Nietzsche argued that when the (master-moralist) Romans took over what is now Israel, a number of low-status Jewish people who were then subjected to Roman rule (the 'slaves') invented Christianity as it valued the weak, the slaves, and thereby devalued the Roman masters and their master morality of courage, strength, pride, etc.
      - E.g. In *Matthew 5* (Sermon on the Mount): 'Blessed are the meek, for the they shall inherit the earth.'
  - Christianity, as a slave revolt against the Romans, introduced a morality which empowered the weak but devalued the strong:
    - 'Suppose the abused, oppressed, suffering, unfree, those uncertain of themselves and weary should moralize: what would their moral evaluation have in common? ... here it is that pity, the kind and helping hand, the warm heart, patience, industriousness, humility, friendliness come into honour ... virtually the only means of enduring the burden of existence.' – *Beyond Good and Evil*, §260
- Christianity was so successful that its morality became ingrained in western culture as the only morality (all else was 'evil').
- But compassion for Nietzsche can be harmful to the power of the human species, as we have only evolved our complexity through hardship. Compassion sustains and proliferates the weak thereby emasculating the human race, and hindering its fruition (the *Übermensch*).
- Therefore from the perspective of the strong, and from the human race in general, compassion is not a value.
  - And of course there is no objective perspective.
- As a consequence, even Schopenhauer presupposed a theological, Christian principle in his descriptive ethics.

If 'God is dead', as Nietzsche famously put it, one has no right to Christian morality, neither prescriptively (Kant) nor descriptively (Schopenhauer).

IX

Schopenhauer and the Mind

Key Point:

Subjectivity cannot 'emerge' from matter, as matter is nothing but a human representation of subjectivity, or 'will'.

- This view argued by Arthur Schopenhauer (1788–1860) is part of a developed philosophical system that can contribute to contemporary discussions of consciousness.

Preamble:

- In his book, *The Character of Consciousness* (2010, Oxford), David Chalmers argues that a sufficient materialist explanation of consciousness will prove impossible. In its stead, Chalmers advocates what he calls *Type-F Monism*:

    o 'Type-F Monism is the view that consciousness is constituted by the intrinsic properties of fundamental physical entities ... phenomenal or protophenomenal properties are located at the fundamental level of physical reality and in a certain sense underlie physical reality itself ... If so, then consciousness and physical reality are deeply intertwined ... the view can be seen as a sort of idealism' (pp.133/4).

Following his advocacy of such an idealism (as opposed to Materialism or Dualism), he writes:

    o 'Overall, Type-F monism promises a deeply integrated and elegant view of nature. No one has yet developed any sort

of detailed theory in this class, and it is not clear whether
such a theory can be developed.' (p.137)

- In fact, such a view of nature has been developed in detail and
  constitutes Schopenhauer's Transcendental Idealism.

  o Chalmers informed me that he had never studied
    Schopenhauer, a common negligence despite
    Schopenhauer's influence on Einstein, Schrödinger,
    Nietzsche, Freud and other influential thinkers.
  o In fact, Erwin Schrödinger, a founder of quantum
    physics, who received the Nobel Prize in Physics in this
    very institution [Stockholm University], was an ardent
    Schopenhauerian.

So I here aim to introduce the relevant parts of Schopenhauer's philosophy so
to see how it bears on modern approaches to the 'science of consciousness'.

What is Matter?

- Nothing but force: repulsion, attraction: the cause of change.

- (Today: repulsion=electromagnetism; attraction = gravity,
  electromagnetism, strong and weak nuclear forces)

- And that is repulsion and attraction of other 'matter', i.e. force.

  o Thus matter is force-on-force.
  o And this is causality.
    ▪ i.e. matter = force = causality

- This identification of matter pre-empts Einstein's matter-energy
  conflation by almost a century ($E=mc^2$).

What is Force?

- Schopenhauer makes clear that for materialists, 'force' is a
  qualitates occultae, an occult, secret quality.

  o Forces are given as an axiom for explanation rather than
    something that can be explained.
    ▪ i.e. for materialists, a sufficient explanation is a
      reduction to occult, unknown 'forces'.

- • (Furthermore, we only know these distinct forces through induction, and so many more could exist of which we are unaware.)

- – Therefore, even if, *per impossibile*, consciousness were 'explained' by materialism, it would be incomplete:
  - o the forces would remain as mysterious as the mystery explained thereby!

Schopenhauer demystifies force to the extent that he provides an additional aspect for which 'force' can be understood:

- – *Firstly*, our understanding of force as matter is a mere idiosyncrasy of our evolution:
  - o (And Schopenhauer advocated evolution in 1818, forty-one years before Darwin's *Origin of Species* was published. Though the theory of evolution dates back to at least the 5th century BC with Empedocles.)
  - o If we were reduced to a submicroscopic size, we would not perceive the same forces as solid matter.
  - o If we represented certain electromagnetic wave frequencies as sound rather than colour, our representation of reality would not be one of material solidity.
    - ▪ And there is no absolute reason why electromagnetic light frequencies should be represented as colour.

- – If we experienced the speed of time more slowly, we would perceive what we call motion as solidity.
  - o The orbit of a planet could appear as a solid ring, for example.
  - o And there is no absolute speed of time with which one could determine material solidity, which is repulsion, a force.
    - ▪ Schopenhauer inherits from Kant this notion that time is *a priori*, not absolute.

Thus firstly our understanding of force is conditioned by our human mental apparatus.

- *Secondly*, and more importantly, we each have an additional understanding of force through ourselves:
    - *Inner subjectivity*
        - For Schopenhauer this includes *Reason*, *Understanding* and *Will*; but it is *Will* that provides the complement to our knowledge of force.
        - *Reason* forms abstract concepts.
        - *Understanding* automatically provides a spatio-temporal conceptual framework for our experience which is pre-rational (from Kant's Transcendental Idealism).
        - *Will* is the primal drive that includes our feelings, all of which are ultimately reducible to pleasure and pain in relation to willed objects, often subconsciously (anticipating Nietzsche).

- We are each a unified, systematic force that has two means of knowledge:
    - = *Double-Aspect Theory*:
        - Sensory-intellectual (3rd-person)
        - Subjective (1st-person)

- *Note*: this is a theory that includes 'vital force', a notion Schopenhauer defends by stating that the accusation that such a force is occult and unverifiable is an accusation also applicable to the forces of nature to which the materialist accusers should like to reduce the organism.
    - An organism cannot be sufficiently explained by the known forces of nature (which today number four). A sufficient explanation requires further forces that subsume the lower in a hierarchy. An organism is an example of such a subsuming force.
    - As Werner Heisenberg noted,
    'it will probably be necessary for an understanding of life to go beyond quantum theory and to construct a new coherent set of concepts, to which physics and chemistry may belong … the combination of Darwin's theory with physics and chemistry would not be sufficient to explain organic life … We would, in spite of the fact that the physical events in the brain belong to the psychic phenomena, not expect

that these could be sufficient to explain them.' – *Physics and Philosophy*

- So, the force that is our action is doubly cognized: bodily motion (behaviour) and *Will.*
  - o (Simultaneously, not causally – Schopenhauer rejected *Free Will.*)

Only in ourselves as a unified system/organism, do we have this double knowledge: we represent our felt *Will* as behaviour.

- For our knowledge of others, such double knowledge is impossible:
  - o We represent others as matter in motion (thus ultimately as force).
    - ▪ i.e. single-aspect (third-person)
  - o We cannot have the same numerical feel of another person, we can only assume it by analogy or instinct.
    - ▪ This is the 'Problem of Other Minds'.

- Now, if we assume that the force that is another's behaviour exists for them also as subjectivity (1st-person), then we can assume that:
  - o All force has for itself a subjectivity.
  - o (This cannot be *proved* because 'proof' means third-person experience, and we cannot by definition have third-person sensory experience of subjectivity.)
  - o As it is unperceivable and immeasurable, it is unscientific (to today's empirical science at least).
  - o But this is a truth beyond science, a *'Philosophical Truth'* as Schopenhauer calls it, which places metaphysics above physics.

- Thus the world is only force, or *Will*, represented by us humans as 'dead matter' (acted upon by force).
  - o Even gravity has an internal Will which we represent as its behaviour (i.e. spatio-temporality) just as we represent human behaviour and assume that there is a corresponding subjective Will.

In sum, *to all force there is a subjective aspect.*

- Therefore we can view *The World as Will and Representation.*

- o   The name of Schopenhauer's main work.
- o   i.e. the ultimate fabric of the world is force or energy or will, which can represent other wills as material objects, or in whatever mode at all.
- –   As force/matter, or matter-energy, already contains, or is, subjectivity (at the minimum a non-rational striving) it is an error to ask how subjectivity emerges from the brain, matter.
  - o   'Matter' already has subjectivity: indeed it is for us the representation of subjectivity for itself.
  - o   Matter is the first-aspect representation of second-aspect Will. They are identical, though not identical in terms of matter (as in *eliminative materialism*).

Thus Schopenhauer presents a *metaphysical ontological Monism* with an *epistemological Dualism*.

- –   i.e. a form of *Transcendental Idealism*, *Identity Theory*, and so-called *Type-F Monism*.

- –   This Monism begins to explain why there are neural correlates of consciousness, and why such correlation does not entail Materialism.
  - o   Mind does not emerge from matter; matter emerges as such from (human) minds.
  - o   Therefore the 'Hard Problem of Consciousness' is hard because the explanatory tools are insufficient:
    - ▪   Employing current science to explain consciousness is analogous to employing Christian theology to explain the cosmos:
      - •   *The ontology is irreducible to the epistemology.*
    - ▪   That 'one day' empirical science will be able to explain consciousness is *faith*.
      - •   Just as Newtonians thought they could explain the odd orbit of Mercury 'one day' using Newtonian physics, so do many scientists today think of today's physics explaining consciousness.
      - •   As Richard Feynman noted,
        'It was a shocking discovery of course

> that Newton's laws are wrong … we now have a much more humble point of view of our physical laws – everything can be wrong.' – *Feynman Lectures on Physics*, v1, ch. 16.

- It took a paradigm shift (*viz.* Relativity) to (better) explain Mercury's orbit with a new set of explanatory tools, axioms.

- So a further paradigm shift is required to better explain consciousness.

- And this new paradigm will, if Schopenhauer had his way, include subjectivity *not as something to be explained by other forces but rather as an aspect of force itself employed to explain reality.*

- For example, the difference between a *motive* and a *mechanical cause*, that is, between a *final cause* and an *efficient cause*, is not that the former is reducible to the latter, but that they are respectively the two forms of knowledge (double-aspect) of the same thing (*Will*/Force with Intent).
  - All forces strive internally, which we represent as spatio-temporal causal mechanical forces.
    - 'Intentionality' is the reflection of Mechanism.

- Schopenhauer therefore advocates a *Natural Teleology*, which he is emphatic in separating from theology, as an atheist.
  - A conflation due to the Enlightenment rejection of all things associated with theology.

- Schopenhauer accepted evolution, but would disagree with its mechanist presuppositions:
  - i.e. evolution as proactive rather than reactive (as there are internal ends, not merely external physical reactions). This is perhaps a form of Lamarckism, but so arguably is the new science of epigenetics.

Schopenhauer's interpreted his own ontology as Pessimism:

- 'The basis of all willing … is need, lack and hence pain … If, on the other hand, it lacks objects of willing, because it is at once deprived of them again by too easy a satisfaction, a fearful emptiness and boredom come ... life swings like a pendulum to and fro between pain and boredom' – *The World as Will and Representation*, vol.1, §57

–   He therefore promoted an ascetic life, one where the will is denied so to halt this inevitable suffering.

–   However, this pessimistic interpretation is not necessary.

–   Friedrich Nietzsche (1844 – 1900) accepted Schopenhauer's metaphysics but revalued and thus renamed its central tenet:
    o   For Schopenhauer, the Will was a *will-to-survive*; for Nietzsche the Will was the *will-to-power* (*Wille zur Macht*).
        ▪   The fundamental thing-in-itself is a striving for power not survival.
        ▪   Survival is nothing but the *lowest degree* of such a will to power.

–   For Schopenhauer, any transcendence of survival caused suffering and was thus to be considered (descriptively) immoral.
    o   Nietzsche valued suffering as a necessary element of power development ("what doesn't kill you makes you stronger"), especially in terms of evolution.
        ▪   Without obstacles that caused suffering in our evolutionary past we would not be the complex, powerful species we are today.

–   Nietzsche considered Schopenhauer's devaluation of suffering and valuation of compassion to be a subconscious Christian presupposition Schopenhauer had, an unwitting 'slave morality'.

–   By considering western morality, a legacy of Christianity, as itself a power structure a form of the *will to power*, Nietzsche offered an interpretation of Schopenhauer's philosophy that was *optimistic*: reality was not to be condemned.

–   For Nietzsche, the *World is Will to Power and Representation*.
    o   (Representation for our power: we only represent that which we can employ for our power ends.)

In conclusion, if we accept the Monism of Schopenhauer and Nietzsche, we can consider subjectivity as an intrinsic part of the represented world-as-matter, a representation evolved for its power utility.

But the explanation of evolution is conditioned not simply by external mechanism (physics) but by the internal will to power (metaphysics), which mechanism is but the third-person phenomenon.

X

The Will to Power

The *will to power* is a central tenet of Friedrich Nietzsche's mature philosophy. I shall seek to outline it through four aspects: the **ontological**, the **organic**, the **psychological**, and the **societal**.

Ontological Aspect of the Will to Power

Nietzsche disavowed the mechanistic pre-Einsteinian physics of his age sired by Newton. Instead, he argued that what was called *matter* was, in fact, a representation of force, or energy. This was informed by his readings of Schopenhauer and Bošković amongst others, and inspired by Heraclitus: *all is force against force, nothing more.*

Now, the physics of his age, and the general physics of today, consider only the *objective* aspect of matter-energy – the relational properties accessible to all. Following especially the arguments of Schopenhauer, Nietzsche asserted that there is also a subjective aspect to energy – that is, a subjectivity. This subjectivity is not consciousness as such, it is rather akin to a feeling, a desire, a drive – a *Will*.

All forces, which are listed today as being of four types, in their subjective aspect, *are* this Will. This Will does *not add* to the force, it *is* the force understood from within.

Now, Schopenhauer considered this Will to be the *will to survive*, to maintain itself in its phenomenal differentiation. Nietzsche advances the theory, so that the Will becomes *not* the *will to survive* but the *will to power*.

The subjective element of energy is a striving to assimilate more energy to its purpose, to its *telos* – that is its power. Thus, the will to power is a *teleological principle* that underlies everything. Everything strives for power, for the most subconsciously.

Though teleological, the will to power is *not* a libertarian principle. That is, Nietzsche is *not* advocating *free will*. The will to power is not free. In fact, Nietzsche rejects free will along with the determinist mechanism, because consciousness does not cause actions, but merely accompanies them.

To be concise: all is force; force has a subjectivity; that subjectivity is a striving for development – a *will to power*.

> *All mechanical events, in so far as an energy is active in them, are really the energy of the will ... [we] designate all effective energy unequivocally as: the will to power. The world as it is seen from the inside, the world defined and described by its 'intelligible character' is simply the 'will to power' and that alone.*
> (*Beyond Good and Evil*, §36)

Organic Aspect of the Will to Power

From this ontological aspect of will to power derives the organic aspect. In fact: *'Life is merely a special case of the will to power.'* (*The Will to Power*, §692)

Schopenhauer and many today believe that the *will to survive* – the survival instinct – is the ultimate drive of all organic beings. For Nietzsche, the will to survive is merely *the lowest degree* of the all-encompassing will to power (see *Beyond Good and Evil*, §13).

If an organism is threatened it will defend itself, but only because its death would end its power. If a being is not threatened it would seek to develop, to advance, to grow, to gain power. This is not greed; this is growth – this is reality.

The will to power does not, of course, merely apply to humans and other animals, but also plants, fungi, and all else. A tree would seek to grow its roots and gain resources just as a person would seek to develop his health, strength, wealth, and status.

> *Life itself, in its essence, means: appropriating, injuring, overpowering those foreign and weaker; oppression, harshness, forcing one's own forms on others, incorporation, and at the very least and the very mildest, exploitation ... Life simply is the will to power.* (*Beyond Good and Evil*, §259)

Now, an individual organism (so-called) may gain power by entering into a symbiotic relationship with other powers – especially if it is relatively weak. The power of the whole increases the power of the constituents therein.

For instance, bacteria can gain advantages by living symbiotically with a human being who is also thereby advantaged. Further, a human being may gain advantage by being part of a group – family, tribe, state, religion, ideology, etc. It is here where characteristics such as compassion, courtesy, generosity, empathy, etc., can play their part. But, always, ultimately, for the power of the group and the individuals who are therein united.

For Nietzsche, a human being, in himself, is already a *multiplicity* of wills to power. Ideally, one Will would dominate giving style, harmony, and direction thereto (see *The Joyous Science*, §290). Incidentally, in this respect, Nietzsche also moves away from Schopenhauer, as the latter considered an organism to be a single Will rather than a multiplicity. For Nietzsche, an organism is a hierarchy.

Nietzsche believed in evolution, but he rejected Darwin's version of evolution. He considered it reactive rather than proactive. That is to say that he considered Darwin to presuppose the essence of a life form to be a will to survive that merely reacts and adapts to its environment rather than proactively seeking to dominate its environment and thereby empowering its species. Moreover, Nietzsche advocated *soft inheritance*, the inheritance of acquired characteristics, rather than the pure neo-Darwinist theory of *hard inheritance* – the former of which is now re-emerging under the name *epigenetics*.

It is important to note that the *will to power* is not some vitalistic, spiritual principle that exists in addition to a body. Rather, it is *numerically identical* to the body, but known immanently. It is ontologically one with the body, but epistemically distinct.

Psychological Aspect of the Will to Power

Our ultimate *telos*, then, is power – not pleasure, not knowledge, not fellowship with a god.

For Nietzsche, most pleasure is an after-effect, a by-product of overcoming an obstacle – that is, of overpowering an obstacle; be that an enemy, an examination, a phobia, a fear, anything that stands in one's way. Although people may *consciously* believe they are acting in order to ultimately attain pleasure or happiness, it is not consciousness that causes one to act, it is will – *will to power*.

Note that, in contrast to most thinkers today, Nietzsche argued that *pain*, in fact, was not to be devalued. Obstacles cause pain, and only through obstacles can we advance our power. Without obstacles and pain, we would not have evolved into the powerful, complex organisms we are today. Pain is necessary for life. It makes life more advanced. As Nietzsche famously stated, *'What doesn't kill you makes you stronger.'* (*Twilight of the Idols*, Maxims, §8).

So, it is not consciousness that causes actions. In fact, human consciousness itself is a *product* of the *will to power*. We only perceive that which was of power importance to us, our ancestors. We are mostly blind to the majority of reality which plays little role in our power. This is parallel to Henri Bergson's thought.

Most of our actions are performed subconsciously. One is not conscious of one's legs' intricate motions when walking, for example. The main role of consciousness is to present to the Will (or Wills) possible actions *vis-à-vis* their consequences. The Will then determines the action by which action offers the most power. Being prudent employs consciousness, but one is still determined by the Will which seeks power.

The *will to power* is subjective, but it is not the same as human consciousness. Very seldom do we become conscious of our true nature.

The *will to truth*, the desire for knowledge, is again subsumed under the *will to power*. Often, gaining knowledge is a means to gaining power. As Francis Bacon stated, *'Knowledge is power.'* But not always is this the case: often a falsity would serve us better. A cult's dogmas, for example, may deliver more power to the leaders and followers than if the members acknowledged their falsity.

In fact, virtually, all our beliefs are false. We merely believe what is in our interest, our power interest. There are exceptions, but these are rare. To begin with, our consciousness already delivers us distorted presentations of reality. Our senses are biased. Consequently, Nietzsche is known as a *Perspectivist*, because beliefs are based on perspectives of power, albeit subconsciously.

A person who feels enslaved will value freedom, as its manifestation would yield power to that person. A person who has more power may value justice as this can be used to earn him ascendance over those more powerful. A person with overflowing power may value the love of humanity as it is, for him, his body of control (see *The Will to Power*, §784).

Indeed, a person of power would be courteous and friendly, and may genuinely love his enemies as they present means, obstacles, for him to test his strength. A lion would not be angered over a mouse; his relative power is too great. Defensiveness betrays weakness.

Well-meaning, helpful, good-natured attitudes of mind have not come to be honoured on account of their usefulness, but because they are states of richer souls that are capable of bestowing and have their value in the feeling of the plenitude of life. (The Will to Power, §932).

Religious belief, for the most part, is a perspective based on subconscious power considerations. Nietzsche singles out Christianity which for him is a perspective of the weak. It offers metaphysical punishment to one's enemies as a real physical punishment is not an option. It offers an afterlife of eternal peace, only a value to someone who suffers from life. It offers a *slave morality* of virtues that benefit the weak – compassion, humility, servility, equal rights, etc. – and presents them as objective, absolute.

Christianity is, itself, a power structure originating in an underclass of the Romans, the latter having a different morality based on their perspective of relative power.

All morality is false – or, rather, no morality is absolute or objective. In this, Nietzsche echoes the arguments of the ancient Sophists whom Plato sought to refute, unsuccessfully in Nietzsche's eyes. All characteristics have had their days as virtues or vices depending on whether they served the power of their subjects. Even violence was a virtue in Homeric Greece.

Societal Aspect of the Will to Power

The danger of Christianity, and the slave morality it has spread, is, from Nietzsche's own perspective, that it values the weak and mediocre over the great and as such has halted humanity's power progress.

Christianity's legacy is so ingrained within western culture that alleged atheists even presuppose this perspective's valuation unwittingly. For example, Utilitarians, such as J.S. Mill, simply assume as axiomatic that pleasure is of higher value than pain, and that each person should have equal rights when calculating the consequences of an action. Likewise, socialists believe in equality as axiomatic without being able to prove why it is an objective value. For Nietzsche, socialism is tantamount to Christianity without the god. But, without the god, there is no sanctioning of this 'slave moral'.

When Nietzsche stated that *'God is dead'*, he meant that if one does not believe in God one has no logical right to believe in the morality which this deity ushered in (see *The Joyous Science*, §343 (and §108 and §125). We

must develop and start thinking in terms *'beyond good and evil'* – the name
of one of his later books.

To conclude: the *will to power* is the fundamental force of all reality. We
observe this power as activity around us, but we can feel this power only
within ourselves. In its epistemic immanence, it is not spatial and so cannot
be measured as such; but, in its objectivity, it is the world and cosmos of
which we are a part.

– Addendum –

The *Metaphysical* Aspect of Nietzsche's Will to Power

The view here advocated, the traditional view, is that Nietzsche contends
all 'matter' to be ultimately force (*Kraft*), and all force to be the outer
representation of an inner *affect*: the will to power (*Wille zur Macht*). As this
immanent aspect to all force cannot be understood solely as physical, the
doctrine is thus *metaphysical*.

It is maintained that this metaphysical doctrine was not completed due to
Nietzsche's cognitive ruination in 1889.

In 1990 the Nietzsche scholar Maudemarie Clark published *Nietzsche
– Truth and Philosophy*, wherein she argued *against* this traditional
interpretation of Nietzsche's will to power as a metaphysical doctrine – a
denial that triggered a considerable following. We shall here present criticism
of her main arguments, a criticism that seeks to maintain the metaphysical,
or cosmological, standing of Nietzsche's central tenet, in defiance of Clark's
legacy.

Clark's initial move is to say that we should ignore the passages on the
will to power from Nietzsche's notebooks because they were unpublished,
and so look at the published works, with special attention to *Beyond Good
and Evil* (BGE) §36. Then, with regard to this pivotal section, she argues that
Nietzsche is not advocating a metaphysical doctrine of the will to power,
despite appearances to the contrary, but is in fact *putting forward a thesis
which he does not believe to be the case*. She argues that Nietzsche is playing
with the reader, putting on a mask in line with his view that *'every deep spirit
needs a mask'* (BGE§40).

The first cause for concern is Clark's dismissive attitude to the notebooks
of 1883–88, commonly referred to as the *Nachlass*. Because Nietzsche was
developing his doctrine of the will to power – as the proposed name of his

never-completed book indicated (see his *Genealogy*, T3, §27, and below) – then that development would only be found in his late notebooks. Furthermore, the notion that the posthumous notes on the will to power principle were his sister's fabrications is highly implausible. Elisabeth Förster-Nietzsche was no philosopher. The educationalist Rudolph Steiner was employed by Elisabeth Förster-Nietzsche at the Nietzsche Archives in 1896. Steiner there gave her introductory lessons in philosophy, but had a very low opinion of her philosophical capabilities. He left a year later. Elisabeth could barely understand Nietzsche's thinking, let alone could she contribute tens of passages on metaphysics. A ten-point defense of the published *Nachlass* book, *The Will to Power* (WP) can be found in the footnote.[1]

The further importance of the *Nachlass* is implied in a letter to another of Nietzsche's friends, Franz Overbeck (who never allowed Nietzsche's sister to acquire his letters). In this correspondence dated 7th April 1884, Nietzsche writes:

> *If I get to Sils Maria this summer I want to undertake a revision of my metaphysical and my epistemological views. ... I am resolved to devote the next five years to the construction of my "philosophy," for which I have in my Zarathustra constructed a vestibule.*

Nietzsche here explicitly indicates his desire to revise his metaphysics, which considered from 1884 and the more Naturalist philosophy of his mid-period, suggests a move away from Naturalism (physics, mechanism). He also refers to his book *Thus Spake Zarathustra* as being a mere 'vestibule' to his revised forthcoming "philosophy". BGE was published in 1886 and so suggests that the 'five years' of the development of his philosophy were not exhausted in that book. Hence more reason to consult the developing thought within his notebooks.

Moreover the *Nachlass* contains more than a hundred sections on the will to power principle. This lights untenable Clark's claim that BGE§36 was nothing but a trivial masked game for his readers.

Secondly, Clark's anti-metaphysical interpretation is at odds with comments within his published works. In his autobiography, *Ecce Homo* (1888), Nietzsche describes BGE thus:

> *This book (1886) is in all essentials a critique of modernity,*
> *the modern sciences ... All the things of which the age is*
> *proud are felt ... almost as bad manners, for example its*
> *celebrated "objectivity" ... its "scientificality".*

Ecce Homo here obviously presents Nietzsche's aversion to Scientism and, by implication, his embrace of metaphysical possibility – thereby annulling Clark's mission. When Nietzsche attacks metaphysics in his mature work, he attacks specific doctrines rather than metaphysics *per se*. This distinction Clark conflates.

Thirdly, it seems that Clark also conflates 'will' with 'free will'. The latter meaning that consciousness originates actions, the former, for Nietzsche, means a *non-conscious* yet *affective striving* underlying all force. Clark confuses this critical distinction when she writes, *'[t]he ultimate causes of our actions, then, are not the conscious thoughts and feelings with which Nietzsche claims we identify the will. Given these passages [BGE§§3, 19], we cannot reasonably attribute to Nietzsche the argument of BG 36'*. But BGE§36 does *not* argue that the immanent aspect of will to power is the *consciousness that originates actions* (*free* will), so the attribution can be made without incoherence to previous passages in BGE. In BGE§21, Nietzsche writes:

> *Now, if someone can see through the cloddish simplicity*
> *of this famous "free will" and eliminate it from his mind,*
> *I would then ask him to take his "enlightenment" a step*
> *further and likewise eliminate ... "unfree will" ... in*
> *conformity with the prevalent mechanistic foolishness that*
> *pushes and tugs ... The "unfree will" is mythology: in real*
> *life it is only a matter of strong and weak wills.*

That is, free will and mechanistic determinism are both errors. Consciousness does not originate actions, and the mechanism in physics does not sufficiently explain reality. In reality there are a multiplicity of wills to power, their differing strength determining action – a non-mechanistic determination. In the *Nachlass*, Nietzsche words this in the following manner:

> *'...no things remain but only dynamic quanta, in a relation*
> *of tension to all other dynamic quanta: their essence lies in*

> *their relation to all other quanta, in their "effect" upon the*
> *same. The will to power not a being, not a becoming, but*
> *a pathos – the most elemental fact from which a becoming*
> *and effecting first emerge.'* (WP§635, March-June 1888)

This section was written in 1888 and thus offers a view on the development of his power project. As it reveals, the will to power underlies all actions and involves a 'pathos': a feeling. That Clark can deny this metaphysical aspect of the will to power is unjustifiable revisionism.

Clark writes, *'Nietzsche encourages us to continue to think in causal terms ... but to abandon the interpretation of causality we derive from our experience of willing. BG 36 therefore gives us no reason to retain belief in the causality of the will, nor any way of reconciling its argument with Nietzsche's repeated rejection of that causality.'* But again, Nietzsche's argument in BGE§36 does *not* involve causality of the will in this Libertarian sense. The will is not of necessity connected to the conscious "I" that believes it controls; the will is mostly subconscious, but it is nonetheless an immanent sentience underlying all energy. It is thus a metaphysical principle, as Nietzsche repeatedly makes clear.

Again, the *Nachlass* provides elaboration of Nietzsche's thinking here. He writes in March-June 1888,

> *... the will to power is the primitive form of affect [Affekt-*
> *Form] ... all driving force is will to power, that there is*
> *no other physical, dynamic or psychic force except this.'*
> (WP§688)

This passage alone hammers Clark's argument. When she writes, *'[the] problem is that if willing is not conscious, it becomes impossible to understand how BG 36 would support its first premise: that only willing is "given," and that we cannot get up or down to any world beyond our drives'*, she betrays the fact that *she does not distinguish consciousness from affect.* The experience of will is not of necessity conscious; shades of differentiation of sentience must be fathomed here.

Furthermore, from the *Nachlass* in 1885:

> *There is absolutely no other kind of causality than that of*
> *will upon will. Not explained mechanistically.'* (WP§658)

This obviously refutes Clark's statement above regarding Nietzsche's repeated rejection of the causality experienced in will, and generally her mechanistic revisionism of Nietzsche. This will-experience is, as such, *a posteriori*, contrary to her initial claims that Nietzsche's argument for a metaphysical will to power would have to be conditioned on an *a priori* basis. It is not.

In sum, Nietzsche's argument against free will does not refute his argument that the will to power has an intrinsic aspect, which is causality understood from the inside – somewhat analogous to A. N. Whitehead's cosmology. BGE§36 is no trick.

Fourthly, Clark attempts to make the case that the proposal within BGE§36 of the will to power as metaphysical, or cosmological, would be a contravention of his Perspectivism. What she does not consider, however, is the fact that Nietzsche's Perspectivism is grounded in his notion of the will to power: all perspectives are based on (mostly subconscious) considerations of power. She has inverted Nietzsche's epistemic hierarchy, and in so doing has exposed his Perspectivism to groundlessness. Perspectivism cannot be applied to its own conditions without destruction.

The overall push of Clark's theory, then, is to dethrone the will to power as a metaphysical and as a central tenet of Nietzsche's philosophy, and to see it as a mere derivative part of his philosophy. She states, *'the will to power, [is] a second-order drive that he recognizes as dependent for its existence on other drives, but which he generalizes and glorifies in his picture of life as will to power. The knowledge Nietzsche claims of the will to power belongs to psychology rather than to metaphysics or cosmology.'* Nietzsche directly contradicts this in BGE§23:

> *Until now, all psychology has been brought to a stop by moral prejudices and fears: it has not dared to plumb these depths ... no-one in his thoughts has even brushed these depths as I have, as a morphology and evolutionary theory of the will to power.*

Further, if the will to power was a mere psychological second-order drive, Nietzsche would not announce in his published *Genealogy of Morality* of 1887 that, *'I am preparing: The Will to Power, Attempt at a Revaluation of All Values'* (T3, §27). Why would Nietzsche name the culmination of his thought from the time of his letter to Overbeck, with the name of a mere second-order drive? It is far more plausible that the will to power was conceived by Nietzsche as a central cosmological, metaphysical principle, as sincerely sketched in BGE§36.

Clark and her ilk would like to reject a metaphysical interpretation of Nietzsche's mature thought for an empirical one. For instance, she claims that 'Nietzsche's doctrine of the will to power must be empirical if it is to cohere with his rejection of metaphysics'. But Nietzsche does not reject metaphysics as a whole in his mature work; he returns to metaphysics. Apart from the published texts and Nachlass, the error of Clark's view is further shown in writings by Nietzsche's friends who would have known his sincere philosophy from more than his books. One particularly close acquaintance was Lou Salomé, to whom Nietzsche proposed. In her book *Friedrich Nietzsche in seinen Werken*, she writes:

> we can trace the transitions from his positivistic
> [empiricist] phase of intellectuality to a mystical
> philosophy of will ... Nietzsche's renewed glorification of
> the artist, and metaphysics even, tells us how far he has
> turned towards a new and opposite type of seeker and how
> far he has already distanced himself from the positivistic
> "reality-philosophy babblers" ... Nietzsche's theory of the
> will points to a merging of his former metaphysical views
> ... as a disciple of Schopenhauer.

Salomé's book was published in 1894 and so presents an intimate understanding of Nietzsche's proposed metaphysical character of the will to power, an understanding that predates Elisabeth Förster-Nietzsche's publication of the *Nachlass*, as well as the secondary literature by Alfred Bäumler, Heidegger, *et al.* (to which an empiricist revisionism can be perceived as counteraction).

I would argue, however, that this power principle was not fully developed by the time of Nietzsche's collapse in 1889, which explains the somewhat cautious, conditional style of BGE§36. That caution is not present in the *Nachlass*, and it is mostly there where we find his most advanced thought. In a later letter to Franz Overbeck dated 24th March 1887, the year after BGE's publication, Nietzsche writes:

> there is the hundredweight of this need pressing upon me
> – to create a coherent structure of thought during the next
> five years.

It is this acknowledged incompletion which bequeaths the hypothetical manner of BGE§36, rather than its insincerity, as Clark believes.

More generally, the question as to how Nietzsche himself conceived the will to power is not as important as the question as to whether it approaches a correct understanding of reality, if such an approach is possible. I believe this potential is hindered by Clark's unjustified critique, and further impeded by those following her dismissal. This dismissal of Nietzsche's cosmological will to power is itself, one could argue, a symptom of a structure assimilating and exploiting its environment for its own power: *'the will to power interprets ... interpretation is itself a means of becoming master'* (WP§643, 1885-1886).

> *The victorious concept "force" ... still needs to be completed: an inner will must be ascribed to it, which I designate as "will to power," i.e., as an insatiable desire to manifest power; or as the employment and exercise of power, as a creative drive ... one is obliged to understand all motion, all "appearances," all "laws," only as symptoms of an inner event.*
> (WP§618 / Nachlass 36[31] – 1885)

Chapter Sources

Philosophy and Psychedelic Phenomenology is an amended essay for the American book *Radical Mycology*. In its amended form, as presented in this book, it was published on *Psychedelic Press UK* online (1st January 2015) and subsequently on *Reality Sandwich* (4th March 2015).

Myco-Metaphysics: a Philosopher on Magic Mushrooms was published in the *Psychedelic Press UK* anthology, volume I (1st March 2014), and in the book *Out of the Shadows* (Muswell Hill Press, 2015).

Psychedelic Experience and Empiricism was self-published online (www.philosopher. eu) in 2014.

Bergson and Psychedelic Consciousness was derived and augmented from a lecture for the *Breaking Convention* conference of July 2013 in London. The essay is published as *Interpreting Psychedelic Consciousness through Bergson's Process Philosophy* in the conference's accompanying book *Neurotransmissions: Essays on Psychedelics from Breaking Convention* (2015, London: Strange Attractor Press).

Vertexes of Sentience: Whitehead and Psychedelic Phenomenology was commissioned by the Dutch *Radboud University Nijmegen* under the direction of philosophy Professor Pieter Lemmens for a forthcoming book tentatively named *Philosophy and Psychedelics: Exploring the Logos of Psychedelia.*

Antichrist Psychonaut: Nietzsche and Psychedelics was published in the *Psychedelic Press UK* anthology, volume IV (24th August 2015).

Neo-Nihilism: the Philosophy of Power was an essay written in 2013 and published on *Amazon* and more as an eBook. It has sold continuously since then, becoming an Amazon best seller. It even inspired the recreation of the Marvel superhero, *Karnak*. It is here presented for the first time in print.

The Teutonic Shift from Christian Morality: Kant, Schopenhauer, Nietzsche is a text derived from Sjöstedt-H's notes from his lecture (27-2-2011) at Conway Hall, London for the *South Place Ethical Society*. The talk was published in the Society's journal *Ethical Record* thereafter (April 2011, vol. 116, no. 4, pp. 20–27).

Schopenhauer and the Mind is a text derived from Sjöstedt-H's notes from his lecture at Stockholm University for the *2011 Towards a Science of Consciousness* conference organized by the University of Arizona. He was offered the place by Professor Stuart Hameroff thereof.

The Will to Power is the transcript of a video lecture Sjöstedt-H created in June 2012, after six years of teaching Nietzsche at college. At this time of publication, the video has a count of nearly 200 000 views. It was also published online and in print for the Canadian magazine *Metanoia* (July 2013). But here in this book it includes an addendum emphasizing the metaphysical character of the principle.

Notes

Chapter I: Philosophy and Psychedelic Phenomenology

1. *The Analysis of Matter*, ch. XXXVII
2. 'Neural correlates of the psychedelic state as determined by fMRI studies with psilocybin', *Proceedings of the National Academy of Sciences,* 24-01-2012. Prof. David J. Nutt, *et al*, Imperial College
3. 'Slime mold uses an externalized spatial "memory" to navigate in complex environments', *Proceedings of the National Academy of Sciences,* 24-6-2012. Chris R. Reid *et al*, The University of Sydney
4. *Science and the Modern World,* ch. VI
5. *The Will to Power*, §522
6. *The World as Will and Representation*, v.1, §15
7. Preface to the second edition of the *Critique of Pure Reason*
8. *"Autobiographical Notes"*, in *Albert Einstein: Philosopher-Scientist*
9. E.g. John Hopkins University. http://archive.magazine.jhu.edu/2011/02/bringing-science-back-to-hallucinogens/
10. *A Philosophical Enquiry into the Origin of our Ideas of the Sublime and Beautiful*
11. 'Thir dread commander: He above the rest
In shape and gesture proudly eminent
Stood like a tower; his form had yet not lost
All her original brightness, nor appeared
Less than the archangel ruin'd, and th' excess
Of glory obscured: as when the sun new ris'n
Looks through the horizontal misty air
Shorn of his beams; or from behind the moon
In dim eclipse disastrous twilight sheds
On half the nations; and with fear of change
Perplexes monarchs.'
(*Paradise Lost*, book 1)
12. *Drug harms in the UK: a multicriteria decision analysis*. Prof David J Nutt FMedSci, Leslie A King PhD, Lawrence D Phillips PhD, on behalf of the *Independent Scientific Committee on Drugs* 2010. Published in *The Lancet*, Volume 376, Issue 9752, Pages 1558 - 1565, 6 November 2010
13. *The Second Treatise of Civil Government* (1690), ch. IV, §57

Chapter II: Myco-Metaphysics

1. Ayer on Logical Positivism, *Men of Ideas*, Bryan Magee. BBC. 1978. Available at youtu.be/4cnRJGs08hE?t=7m
2. Ayer, Alfred Jules. What I Saw When I Was Dead. *Sunday Telegraph*, 28ᵗʰ August 1988. www.philosopher.eu/others-writings/a-j-ayer-what-i-saw-when-i-was-dead
3. Osorio D., Zylinski S. Cuttlefish vision in camouflage. *Journal of Experimental Marine Biology and Ecology* 2013, vol. 447.
4. Healy K., McNally L., Ruxtond G. D., Cooper N., Jackson A. L. Metabolic rate and body size are linked with perception of temporal information. *Animal Behaviour* 2013;86(4).
5. Nietzsche F. *The Pre-Platonic Philosophers* (Chicago, IL, 2006), pp. 61–2.
6. Encapsulated best in his *magnum opus*, *Matter and Memory*.

Chapter III: Psychedelics and Empiricism

1. David Hume, *An Enquiry Concerning Human Understanding*, §2
2. *Ibid.*
3. *Ibid.*
4. 'It is readily allowed, that other beings may possess many senses of which we can have no conception; because the ideas of them have never been introduced to us in the only manner by which an idea can have access to the mind, to wit, by the actual feeling and sensation.'(*Ibid.*)
5. '*It is acknowledged, that, in fact, many of these perceptions arise not from anything external, as in dreams, madness, and other diseases. And nothing can be more inexplicable than the manner, in which body should so operate upon mind as ever to convey an image of itself to a substance, supposed of so different, and even contrary a nature. It is a question of fact, whether the perceptions of the senses be produced by external objects, resembling them: how shall this question be determined? By experience surely; as all other questions of a like nature. But here experience is, and must be entirely silent. The mind has never anything present to it but the perceptions, and cannot possibly reach any experience of their connexion with objects. The supposition of such a connexion is, therefore, without any foundation in reasoning.*' (*Ibid.* §12)
6. More strictly, innate ideas with which potential of realising non-experientially we are born.

Chapter IV: Bergson and Psychedelic Consciousness

1. *The Analysis of Matter*, ch. XXXVII, p. 389
2. p. 10

3. M. Gagliano, *et al.* (2014) Experience teaches plants to learn faster and forget slower in environments where it matters. *Oecologia*, vol. 175 (May, Issue 1) pp. 63-72

4. Chris R. Reid *et al.* (2012) Slime mold uses an externalized spatial "memory" to navigate in complex environments. *Proceedings of the National Academy of Sciences of the United States of America*, vol. 109 (October, no. 43, 17490–17494)

5. *Science and the Modern World*, ch. VI, p.103

6. *Creative Evolution*, ch. IV, p. 266

7. *Creative Evolution*, ch. IV, p. 267

Chapter V: Vertexes of Sentience

1. *Modes of Thought*, ch.s III … IX.

2. As David Hume argued with his Problem of Induction: 'it implies no contradiction, that the course of nature may change' (*An Enquiry Concerning Human Understanding*, §4, pt 2). Whitehead makes the same point when he writes, '[S]tatistics tell you nothing about the future unless you make the assumption of the permanence of statistical form. ...There is no valid inference from mere possibility to matter of fact, or, in other words, from mere mathematics to concrete nature.' (*Adventures of Ideas*, ch. VIII)

3. *Modes of Thought*, ch. VIII

4. See William James' *A Pluralistic Universe*.

5. Patrizi coined the term 'panpsychism'.

6. E.g. Aristotle's *pneuma*.

7. *Process and Reality*, Part II, ch. III, §I, p.87

8. *Process and Reality*, Part V, ch. II, §II, p.344

9. 'The concrescence is dominated by a subjective aim … This subjective aim is this subject itself determining its own self-creation as one creature.' (*Process and Reality*, Part II, ch. II, §2, p.69)

10. *Process and Reality*, Part II, ch. I, §V, p.50

11. *Ibid.* Also known as 'objectification' (*ibid.*).

12. In his book *Matter and Memory*.

13. *Religion in the Making*, ch. VII

14. *Ibid.*

15. *Ibid.*

16. Or, more strictly, 'scientism'.

17. *The World as Will and Representation*, ch. XVIII

18. *Process and Reality*, Part II, ch. IV, §5, p.119

19. *Science and the Modern World*, ch. VI

20. *Process and Reality*, Part II, ch. I, §VI, p.57

21. *Process and Reality*, Part II, ch. II, §VI, p.80

22. *Process and Reality*, Part II, ch. VI, §III, p.149

23. *Process and Reality*, Part II, ch. VII, §IV, p.164

24. '"[D]ecision" does not here imply conscious judgement…' (*Process and*

Reality, Part II, ch. I, §II, p.43)

25. *Process and Reality*, Part II, ch. III, §I, p.84

26. *Religion in the Making*, ch. III, §VII

27. *Process and Reality*, Part II, ch. III, §II, p.91

28. *Process and Reality*, Part II, ch. III, §IV, p.97

29. *Modes of Thought*, ch. VIII

30. *Process and Reality*, Part II, ch. III, §X, p.106

31. *Process and Reality*, Part II, ch. III, §XI, p.108

32. *Process and Reality*, Part II, ch. III, §XI, p.107

33. *Science and the Modern World*, ch. IX

34. See *Science and the Modern World*, ch. X

35. *Process and Reality*, Part II, ch. VII, §III, p.163

36. *Process and Reality*, Part II, ch. III, §IV, p.98

37. *Process and Reality*, Part II, ch. III, §IX, p.105. Cf. Nietzsche's *Beyond Good and Evil*, §259

38. *Process and Reality*, Part III, ch. III, §I, p.244

39. *Iliad* (Book 19)

40. At least according to a cosmological interpretation of Nietzsche's Eternal Return.

41. Act 3, Scene 1

42. Book II

43. E.g. by Norwegian philologist Sophus Bugge (*Studien*, Munich, 1898)

44. *Process and Reality*, Part II, ch. III, §III, p.96

45. *Process and Reality*, Part V, ch. II, §II, p.343

46. Bertrand Russell, *The Problems of Philosophy*, ch. 9

47. *Process and Reality*, Part V, ch. II, §II, p.344

48. *Process and Reality*, Part V, ch. II, §II, p.344

49. *Process and Reality*, Part II, ch. VII, §IV, p.164

50. *Ibid.*

51. *Process and Reality*, Part II, ch. III, §I, p.88

52. *Process and Reality*, Part V, ch. II, §II, p.345

53. *Process and Reality*, Part V, ch. III, §X, p.105

54. See, for instance, his *Zend-Avesta*, or his *Ueber die Seelenfrage*.

55. *Religion in the Making*, ch. IV, §V

56. The subjective aim allows for a limited Libertarianism.

57. *Religion in the Making*, ch. III, §V

58. *Modes of Thought*, ch. I

59. *Ibid.*

60. *Ecce Homo*, Destiny, §9

61. *Science and the Modern World*, ch. XI

62. *Science and the Modern World*, ch. XII

63. *Process and Reality*, Part II, ch. III, §XI, p.108

64. 'Reason is inexplicable if purpose [final cause] be ineffective ... [a] satisfactory cosmology must explain the interweaving of efficient and of final causation.' (*The Function of Reason*, ch. I)

65. *The Varieties of Religious Experience*, ch. XVI

66. Letter to William James dated 31st March 1910.

67. E.g. Barker S.A., Borjigin J., Lomnicka I., Strassman, R. (Jul 2013). "LC/MS/MS analysis of the endogenous dimethyltryptamine hallucinogens, their precursors, and major metabolites in rat pineal gland microdialysate". *Biomed Chromatogr.* 27 (12): 1690–1700

68. Letter to William James dated 31st March 1910.

69. *Creative Evolution*, ch. I

70. As opposed to the less distinct yet more ubiquitous 'perceptive mode of causal efficacy' of which traditional empiricism is ignorant.

71. *Science and the Modern World*, ch. XIII

72. *An Enquiry Concerning Human Understanding*, §2

73. *Adventures of Ideas*, ch. XIII,

74. *The World as Will and Representation*, Book III, §36

75. *The Will to Power*, §619. Also see *Beyond Good and Evil*, §36. I hold the traditional metaphysical interpretation of Nietzsche's later philosophy, a view defended here: www.philosopher.eu/metaphysical-doctrine-of-nietzsches-will-to-power

76. *The Doors of Perception*, p.12

77. The study of 'The One', as opposed to the study of being (ontology).

78. *A Pluralistic Universe*, ch. VII

79. *The Varieties of Religious Experience*, ch. XVI

80. 'The disastrous separation of body and mind which has been fixed on European thought by Descartes is responsible for this blindness of science.' (*Modes of Thought*, ch. VIII)

81. *Adventures of Ideas*, ch. XIII

82. *Science and the Modern World*, ch. IX

83. *The Long Trip: A Prehistory of Psychedelia*, Introduction, p.27

84. *Creative Evolution*, ch. II, pp.177–178

85. *Creative Evolution*, ch. IV, p.267

86. *Confessions of an English Opium Eater*, pp.236–238

Chapter VI: Antichrist Psychonaut

1. 'Psychedelic' is a term coined in 1957 by psychiatrist Dr Humphry Osmond to emphasise the psychotherapeutic value of certain psychoactive drugs, notably LSD. The etymological conjuncts are *psyche* (mind) and *dēloun* (to reveal), the latter from *dēlos* (visible, clear). I use the term 'psychedelic' broadly in this text to refer to a chemically-induced state of mind that brings forth extraordinary representations.

2. Thomas De Quincey, *Confessions of an English Opium Eater*, pleasures, p. 195. 1821AD.

3. Curtis Cate, p. 13.

4. Paul Deussen, 1859-1864. *Conversations with Nietzsche*, p. 15.

5. *Ecce Homo*, Wise, §1, p. 38.

6. Elisabeth Förster-Nietzsche, *The Life of Nietzsche*, vol. II, ch. XXVII.

7. Paul Deussen, 1859-1864. *Conversations with Nietzsche*, p.10.

8. Paul Deussen, 1859-1864. *Conversations with Nietzsche*, p.15.

9. Letter to Erwin Rohde, 3rd April 1868.

10. Incidentally where Paracelsus is believed to have re-introduced opium (as Laudanum) to Europe in the sixteenth century.

11. Letter to Karl von Gersdorff, 20th October 1870 – my emphases.

12. Arthur Schopenhauer, *Essay on the Freedom of the Will*, ch. III.

13. *The Dionysian Worldview, §1.*

14. *The Dionysian Worldview, §3.*

15. *The Birth of Tragedy, Attempt at a Self-Criticism*, §1, p. 3.

16. *The Birth of Tragedy*, §1, pp. 16-17.

17. *The Birth of Tragedy, Attempt at a Self-Criticism*, §4, pp. 6-7.

18. See Curtis Cate, *Friedrich Nietzsche*, p. 280.

19. Published in January 1883.

20. Letter to Lou Salomé and Paul Rée, mid-December 1882.

21. Lou Salomé, *Friedrich Nietzsche in seinen Werken,* ch. III, p. 144. Also note especially in *Zarathustra* these chapters: *Of Great Events*, the coffin-of-masks nightmare in *The Prophet, The Stillest Hour, Of The Three Evil Things*, and *The Intoxicated Song.*

22. *The Joyous Science*, Book I, §43.

23. *The Joyous Science,* Appendix*, The Mysterious Bark*, p. 359.

24. *The Joyous Science,* Appendix, *Rimus remedium*, p. 365.

25. Lou Salomé, *Friedrich Nietzsche in seinen Werken*, ch. III, p. 145.

26. *Twilight of the Idols*, Maxims, §8, p. 33.

27. 1893, as reported by Heinrich Lec in *Conversations with Nietzsche*, §75, p. 230.

28. Letter to Franz Overbeck, 1st February 1883.

29. Elisabeth Förster-Nietzsche, *The Life of Nietzsche*, vol. II, ch. XXVII.

30. His sister may have had an ulterior motive to promote this narcotic view of the cause of his madness: to dismiss claims that syphilis was to blame (see, e.g., E. F. Podach). But as we see, it was not only his sister who spoke of his excessive use of chloral – and besides, madness onset by ongoing drug abuse is hardly more respectable than student-era brothel debauchery.

31. H. Göring, *Conversations with Nietzsche*, §38, p. 100 – my emphases.

32. See Selina Hastings, *Evelyn Waugh: A Biography.*

33. Oliver Sacks, *Hallucinations*, ch. VI, pp. 115-116.

34. *Conversations with Nietzsche*, §52, p. 164.

35. *Conversations with Nietzsche*, §52, p. 163.

36. See his *Annäherungen: Drogen und Rausch* (*Approaches to Drugs and Intoxication*), 1970. In Nietzsche's *Daybreak*, §575, he refers to himself as an '*aeronaut of the spirit*'.

37. *Gesamtausgabe Band* 90, 227.

38. *Ecce Homo*, Clever, §6.

39. See *On the Genealogy of Morality*, bk I, §2.

40. Charles Baudelaire, *Artificial Paradises*, On Wine and Hashish (1851), §V, p. 23.

41. Curtis Cate, *Friedrich Nietzsche*, ch. 38, p. 541.

42. See William James, *The Varieties of Religious Experience*, ch. XVI.

43. *Ecce Homo*, Zarathustra, §3. See also Nietzsche's description of a philosopher in *Beyond Good and Evil*, §292.

44. Elisabeth Förster-Nietzsche, *The Life of Nietzsche*, vol. II, ch. XXVII.

45. Walter Benjamin sees the lady in this light in his own psychedelic *mescaline* experience: 'From the cracks of the Förster House grow tufts of hair. The Förster House: (she [Elisabeth Förster-Nietzsche] has turned the Nietzsche Archive into a Förster House [forester's lodge]) the Förster house is of red stone.

I am a spindle in its banister: an obdurate, hardened post. But that is no longer the totem pole – only a wretched copy. Chamois' foot or horse's hoof of the devil: a vagina symbol.' (*On Hashish*, ch. XI, 22nd May 1934.)

46. Elisabeth Förster-Nietzsche, *The Life of Nietzsche*, vol. II, ch. XXVII.

47. See Toine Pieters' *Java Coca and the Dutch Narcotics Industry: An Almost Forgotten 20th C. History of Drugs Story:* https://pointsadhsblog. wordpress.com/2012/12/10/java-coca-and-the-dutch-narcotics-industry-an-almost-forgotten-20th-c-history-of-drugs-story/

48. E.g. to Cosima Wagner: 'Ariadne, I love you. – Dionysus' (Early January, 1889). In *Beyond Good and Evil*, §295, (1886) Nietzsche writes, 'Dionysus … once said, "In certain cases I love human beings" (and he was alluding to Ariadne, who was present)…'

49. *The Birth of Tragedy*, Attempt at a Self-Criticism, §5. 1886.

50. *Twilight of the Idols*, Ancients, §5. A Dionysian will thus welcome the 'bad trip', and desire its eternal return.

51. *Beyond Good and Evil*, §295.

Chapter VII – Chapter X
No notes

Chapter XI: The Will to Power

1. *It is often remarked that Nietzsche's collection of notes ('Nachlass') from 1883 to 1888, bound as the book named 'The Will to Power', is without value because it was fabricated by his sister, Elisabeth Förster-Nietzsche, head of the Nietzsche-Archiv in Weimar, after her brother's death.*
However, on the contrary, the book is undoubtedly of value. The following elementary points seek to highlight this fact.

i. The ORDER of Nietzsche's notes was originally directed by Elisabeth Förster-Nietzsche (*et al.*), but the note TEXT itself was written by Friedrich Nietzsche. In fact, the fourfold division of the manuscript was suggested by Nietzsche himself, and the name '*The Will to Power*' was planned by him (e.g. in *Genealogy*, T3, §27; and in a note from 17th march 1887) as a then-forthcoming book title.

ii. In the 1960s, philologists Mazzino Montinari and Georgio Colli called the book a 'historic forgery' because its specific order was not created as a book by Friedrich Nietzsche himself. But, the value of the book, as a collection of Friedrich Nietzsche's thoughts, remains despite this affront at its order.

iii. It was in fact Friedrich Nietzsche's friend, Heinrich Köselitz ('Peter Gast'), who suggested to Elisabeth the idea of publishing the notes as the book.

iv. It was also Köselitz who then became chief 'decipherer' of Friedrich Nietzsche's near-illegible scribblings for the book (he offered his services as such in a letter to Elisabeth dated 6th October 1893). Thus it was Köselitz (and others such as Fritz Koegel and Arthur Seidl) who chiefly transcribed *The Will to Power*, rather than Elisabeth alone.

v. There is no evidence and little reason to believe that Elisabeth Förster-Nietzsche (or others) wrote the actual note text within the book. The expanded version of *The Will to Power*, with its 1067 sections, was expressly edited by Elisabeth and Köselitz/Gast (in 1906), making any forgery by Elisabeth less plausible.

vi. The educationalist Rudolf Steiner was employed by Elisabeth Förster-Nietzsche at the Nietzsche Archives in 1896. Steiner there gave her introductory lessons in philosophy, but had a very low opinion of her philosophical capabilities (see H. F. Peters' 'Zarathustra's Sister', 173). He left a year later. Thus Elisabeth was certainly no philosopher, and thus it is implausible that she contributed passages to pass as her brother's.

vii. There is no question that the writings in *The Will to Power* are genuine. It was always the order and omissions of the book which were disliked by some. As Mazzino Montinari stated: "That Frau Förster-Nietzsche and Peter Gast chose to publish these notes in precisely this way, which is neither correct nor appropriate for the *Nachlass* is, however, the really decisive and serious objection to the whole compilation, much more so than the possible suppression of notes' (*The Malahat Review*, no. 24, Oct 1972).

viii. The rejection of the book's value is often a counteraction to early claims that the book was Nietzsche's *magnum opus* (e.g. by the National Socialist sympathisers Alfred Bäumler and especially Heidegger).
ix. Many, if not most, of the notes were quite obviously used in Nietzsche's published works.

x. Ultimately, whether or not Friedrich Nietzsche stood by these notes, unpublished in his lifetime, is academic (in both senses): the value (or lack thereof) of the text upholds itself regardless of who wrote or published it. Would Darwin's 'On the Origin of Species' or Shakespeare's 'Hamlet' become valueless if we suddenly doubted the authors?

Bibliography

Ansell-Pearson, K. & Mullarkey, J (ed.s) (2002) *Henri Bergson: Key Writings*, London: Continuum

Ayer, A. J. (1936/2001) *Language, Truth and Logic*, London: Penguin

Baudelaire, C. (1857/2010) *The Flowers of Evil* and *Paris Spleen*, New York: Dover

Baudelaire, C. (1860/1996) *Artificial Paradises*, New York: Citadel

Benjamin, W. (1927–34/2006) *On Hashish*, Cambridge: Belknap Press of Harvard University

Bergson, H. (1896/1999) *Matter and Memory*, 6th edition, New York: Zone Books

Bergson, H. (1903/1999) *An Introduction to Metaphysics*, Indianapolis: Hackett

Bergson, H. (1907/1998) *Creative Evolution*, New York: Dover

Bergson, H. (1901–1913/2007) *Mind-Energy*, London: Palgrave Macmillan

Breazeale, D. – *Ecce Psycho: Remarks on the case of Nietzsche* (International Studies in Philosophy XXIII/2)

Burke, E. (1757/2008) *A Philosophical Enquiry into the Origin of our Ideas of the Sublime and Beautiful*, Mineola: Dover Publications, Inc.

Carey, N. (2012) *The Epigenetics Revolution*, London: Icon Books

Cate, C. (2002) *Friedrich Nietzsche*, London: Random House

Chalmers, D. J. (2010) *The Character of Consciousness*, New York: Oxford University Press

Deleuze, G. (1962/1996) *Nietzsche and Philosophy*, London: Athlone

Deleuze, G. (1988/1997) *Bergsonism*, 4th edition, New York: Zone Books

De Quincey, T. (1821/1994) *Confessions of an English Opium Eater*, Ware: Wordsworth Classics

Descartes, R. (1637/1641/1996) *Discourse on Method and Meditations on First Philosophy*, New Haven & London: Yale University

Devereux, P. (1997/2008) *The Long Trip: A Prehistory of Psychedelia*, Brisbane: Daily Grail Publishing

Fechner G. T. (1800s/1946) *Religion of a Scientist* (ed. R. Lowrie), Pantheon

Fechner, G. T. (1848) *Nanna oder das Seelenleben der Pflanzen*

Fechner, G. T. (1851) *Zend-Avesta, Über die Dinge des Himmels und des Jenseits, vom Standpunkt der Naturbetrachtung*

Fechner, G. T. (1861) *Über die Seelenfrage*

Förster-Nietzsche, E. (1915/2007) *The Life of Nietzsche – Volume 2*, The Classics

Freud, S. (1930/2002) *Civilization and Its Discontents*, London: Penguin

Gilman, S. L. (ed.) (1987) *Conversations with Nietzsche*, Oxford: Oxford University Press

Greenfield, R. (2006) *Timothy Leary: A Biography*, Orlando: Harcourt Books

Hartshorne, C. (1997) *The Zero Fallacy*, Illinois: Carus

Hastings, S. (1994). *Evelyn Waugh: A Biography*, London: Sinclair-Stevenson

Heisenberg, W. (1962/2000) *Physics and Philosophy*, London: Penguin

Hume, D. (1748/1993) *An Enquiry Concerning Human Understanding*, 2nd edition, Indianapolis: Hackett

Huxley, A. (1954/56/2004) *The Doors of Perception* and *Heaven and Hell*, London: Vintage

James, W. (1890/1950) *Principles of Psychology, volumes 1 and 2*, New York: Dover.

James, W. (1902/1985) *The Varieties of Religious Experience*, London: Penguin Books Ltd.

James, W. (1909/1996) *A Pluralistic Universe*. Collier

James, W. (1912/1996) *Essays in Radical Empiricism*, University of Nebraska Press

Jünger, E. (1970/1980) *Annäherungen: Drogen und Rausch*, Stuttgart: Klett-Cotta im Ullstein Taschenbuch

Kant, I. (1766/2002) *Dreams of a Spirit-Seer*, Pennsylvania: Swedenborg Foundation

Kant, I. (1781/87/1998) *Critique of Pure Reason*, Cambridge: Cambridge University Press

Kant, I. (1785/2005) *The Moral Law/Groundwork of the Metaphysics of Morals*, New York: Routledge

Kant, I. (1788/2002) *Critique of Practical Reason*, Indianapolis: Hackett

Kant, I. (1797/1996) *The Metaphysics of Morals*, Cambridge: Cambridge University Press

Khazaee, M. K. – *The Case of Nietzsche's Madness* (Existenz, Vol. 3, No. 1, Spring 2008)

Leary, T. Metzner, R. and Alpert, R. (1964/2008) *The Psychedelic Experience*, London: Penguin

Leibniz, G. W. (1686/97/1703–05/14/1991) *Discourse on Metaphysics and Other Essays*, Indianapolis: Hackett

Letcher, A. (2007) *Shroom: A Cultural History of the Magic Mushroom*, New York: HarperCollins

Lippit, J. & Urpeth, J. (ed.s) (2000) *Nietzsche and the Divine*, Manchester: Clinamen Press

Locke, J. (1980) *The Second Treatise of Civil Government*, Indianapolis: Hackett

Michaux, H. (1956/2002) *Miserable Miracle*, New York: New York Review of Books

Middleton, C. (ed.) (1969/1996) *Selected Letter of Friedrich Nietzsche*, Indianapolis: Hackett

Mill, J. S. (1859/2005) *On Liberty*, New York: Cosimo, Inc.

Nagel, T. (1979/2012) *Mortal Questions*, Cambridge, Cambridge University Press

Nicholas, L. G. & Ogamé, K. (2006) *Psilocybin Mushroom Handbook*, Quick American

Nietzsche, F. (1870/1997) *The Dionysian Worldview* (Journal of Nietzsche Studies, No. 13, Spring 1997, pp. 81 – 97)

Nietzsche, F. (1871/1993) *The Birth of Tragedy*, London: Penguin

Nietzsche, F. (1881/1997) *Daybreak*, Cambridge: Cambridge University Press

Nietzsche, F. (1882/1974) *The Gay Science*, New York: Vintage

Nietzsche, F. (1883/1969) *Thus Spoke Zarathustra*, London: Penguin

Nietzsche, F. (1886/2008) *Beyond Good and Evil,* Oxford: Oxford University Press

Nietzsche, F. (1887/1998) *On the Genealogy of Morality*, Indianapolis: Hackett

Nietzsche, F. (1888/2007) *Ecce Homo*, London: Penguin

Nietzsche, F. (1889/1990) *Twilight of the Idols* and *The Antichrist*, London: Penguin

Nietzsche, F. (1906[ph]]/1968) *The Will to Power*, New York: Random House

Nussbaum, M. C. – The Transfigurations of Intoxication: Nietzsche, Schopenhauer, and Dionysus (*Arion: A Journal of Humanities and the Classics*, Third Series, Vo. 1, No. 2, Spring 1991, pp. 75 – 111)

O'Brien, E. (1964) *The Essential Plotinus*, Indianapolis: Hackett

Piper, A. (2015) *Strange Drugs Make for Strange Bedfellows: Ernst Jünger, Albert Hofmann and the Politics of Psychedelics*, Portland: Invisible College Publishing

Powell, S. G. (2015) *Magic Mushroom Explorer: Psilocybin and the Awakening Earth*, Rochester: Park Street Press

Redbeard, R. (1890/2005) *Might is Right*, Springfield: Dil Pickle Press

Russell, B. (1912/1980) *The Problems of Philosophy*, Oxford: Oxford University Press

Russell, B. (1921/2008) *The Analysis of Mind*, Stilwell: Digireads

Russell, B. (1927/2007) *The Analysis of Matter*, Nottingham: Spokesman

Sacks, O. (2012) *Hallucinations*, New York: Random House

Salomé, L. (1894/2001) *Nietzsche*, Illinois: Illinois

Schilpp, P. A. (ed.) (1941) *The Philosophy of Alfred North Whitehead*, Illinois: Northwestern University

Schilpp, P. A. (ed.) (1951) *Albert Einstein: Philosopher-Scientist*, 2nd edition, New York: Tudor

Schopenhauer, A. (1818/1966) *The World as Will and Representation, volume 1*, New York: Dover

Schopenhauer, A. (1839/2005) *Essay on the Freedom of the Will*, Mineola: Dover

Schopenhauer, A. (1844/1966) *The World as Will and Representation, volume 2*, New York: Dover

Schopenhauer, A. (1851/2010) *Parerga and Paralipomena, volume 1*, New York: Oxford University Press

Schopenhauer, A. (1851/2010) *Parerga and Paralipomena, volume 2*, New York: Oxford University Press

Schopenhauer, A. (1839/40/2010) *The Two Fundamental Problems of Ethics*, New York: Oxford University Press

Shanon, B. (2010) *The Antipodes of the Mind: Charting the Phenomenology of the Ayahuasca Experience*, New York: Oxford University press

Skrbina, D. (2007) *Panpsychism in the West*, Cambridge: MIT Press

Spinoza, B. (1677/2001) *Ethics*, London: Wordsworth Classics

Stafford, P. (2003) *Magic Mushrooms*, Oakland: Ronin Publishing

Stevenson, C. L. (1944/1972) *Ethics and Language*, New Haven: Yale University Press

Strassman, R. (2008) *Inner Paths to Outer Space*, Rochester: Park Street Press

Strawson, G. *et al.* (2006) *Consciousness and its Place in Nature: Does Physicalism entail Panpsychism?*, Exeter: Imprint Academic

Watts, A. W. (1962/2013) *The Joyous Cosmology*, Novato: New World Library

Waugh, E. (1957/1973) *The Ordeal of Gilbert Pinfold*, London: Chapman & Hall

Whitehead, A. N. (1920/2004) *The Concept of Nature*, New York: Prometheus

Whitehead, A. N. (1925/1967) *Science and the Modern World*, New York: Free Press

Whitehead, A. N. (1926/2011) *Religion in the Making*, New York: Cambridge University Press

Whitehead, A. N. (1927/1985) *Symbolism: Its Meaning and Effect*, New York: Macmillan Co.

Whitehead, A. N. (1929/1978) *Process and Reality (corrected ed.)*, New York: Free Press

Whitehead, A. N. (1929) *The Function of Reason*, Princeton: Princeton University Press

Whitehead, A. N. (1933/1967) *Adventures of Ideas*, New York: MacMillan.

Whitehead, A. N. (1938/1968) *Modes of Thought*, New York: MacMillan.

Wilson, R. A. (1983/2010) *Prometheus Rising*, Las Vegas: New Falcon Publications

About the Author

Peter Sjöstedt-H is an Anglo-Scandinavian philosopher who specialises in the thought of Schopenhauer, Nietzsche, Bergson and Whitehead, and within the field of Philosophy of Mind. Peter has a Bachelor's degree in Philosophy and a Master's degree in Continental Philosophy from the University of Warwick, where he was awarded a first-class distinction for his dissertation on Kant and Schelling in relation to 'intellectual intuition'. Peter subsequently became a Philosophy Lecturer in South Kensington, London for six years before recently returning to the tranquillity of westernmost Cornwall. He is now pursuing his PhD at Exeter University researching Panpsychism, teaching philosophy modules and essay-writing skills, giving public talks, writing articles, and maintaining his website:

www.philosopher.eu

Psychedelic Press: *A Rhizome of Psychedelics, Writing and Culture*

Psychedelic Press is an independent publisher based in Cornwall, UK, that deals with the science, history and literature of psychoactive substances, and altered states of consciousness.

www.psychedelicpress.co.uk

Made in the USA
Middletown, DE
31 July 2020